Inspira...

Soccer Stories

For Kids

21 Amazing & Motivational True Lessons about Overcoming Challenges and Achieving Goals to Inspire Young Soccer Players and Aspiring Athletes from the best: Lionel Messi, Cristiano Ronaldo, Alex Morgan, Mia Hamm, Kylian Mbappé, and more

By **Lucas Martin**

About the Author

Lucas Martin is a sports enthusiast and a passionate children's book author, especially in the children's soccer niche. Visit www.sportsstoriesforkids.com to get Lucas's Soccer Skills Starter Kit for FREE.

In his books, Lucas shares his knowledge and passion for soccer and the inspiring stories of the greatest soccer players of all time. He turns these lessons into fun and engaging stories that help children develop healthy relationships with themselves, others, and soccer.

In his honest and inspiring books, Lucas discusses the benefits of playing soccer and following your dreams. He shares best practices for helping children develop soccer skills, confidence, teamwork, and sportsmanship. He also guides you to discover, create, and become who you want to be.

A child of British parents and having grown up in Buenos Aires, Argentina, Lucas speaks Spanish and English fluently. When he's not on his mission to change the world, he loves to watch and play soccer with his kids, read, and travel.

In Argentina, he faced many challenges and difficulties to pursue his soccer passion. He was inspired by Messi, who overcame his humble origins and became one of the best soccer players in history. He decided to write in this niche to share Messi's story and values with other children who may face similar challenges and difficulties, and to inspire and empower them to follow their passion and achieve their potential.

Lucas lives in Barcelona, Spain, with his wife and two kids, a girl and a boy, where he enjoys the culture and history of soccer and Messi's career. He's also a huge fan of hockey and basketball, among other sports.

Your Free Gifts

To thank you for your purchase, I'm offering my readers the eBook, *Building Confidence for Kids*, for FREE.

To get instant access, go to:
https://www.sportsstoriesforkids.com/freegift

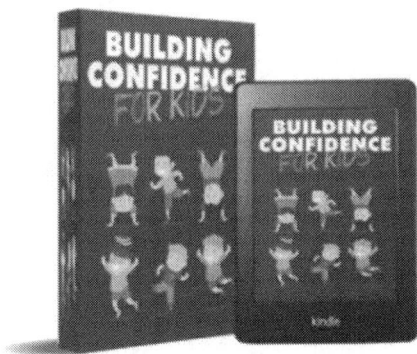

Ready to Raise a Super Confident Kid?

Why this eBook is so essential:

- **Enhance Performance in Sports:** Confidence is critical in sports; it empowers children to believe in their abilities and improves their performance on the field.
- **Growth mindset development**: A confident kid is more inclined towards embodying a growth mindset, meaning they see challenges as opportunities to learn and grow rather than insurmountable obstacles.
- **Long-term Life Skills:** Building confidence helps children develop essential skills such as independence, problem-solving, and decision-making.

This eBook is valued at $5, but it is completely free for you!

And that's not all!

You will also receive a comprehensive collection of parenting eBooks that I've personally curated. These five volumes include parenting guides, self-esteem building, rules and discipline, and practical parenting tips.

This special book bundle is valued at $14,99. But, of course, it is free for you!

Grab the free book and the parenting book bundle for the best advice on raising a confident child.

But there is more! Of course, there is a special gift for your kid too!

Free Gifts For Your Kid

1. <u>FREE E-BOOK</u>

"The Young Player's Playbook: Winning Strategies for Soccer Success: From Basic Drills to Big Dreams – A Soccer Star's Roadmap for Ages 6 to 12"

The ultimate guide to developing soccer skills and confidence-building on and off the field!

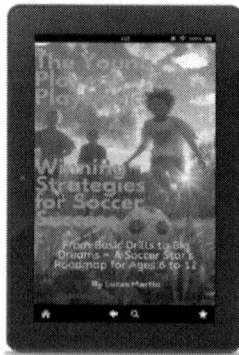

2. <u>LIONEL MESSI'S JOURNEY</u>

- An Inspirational Digital Timeline Poster
- This poster will be a daily source of inspiration!

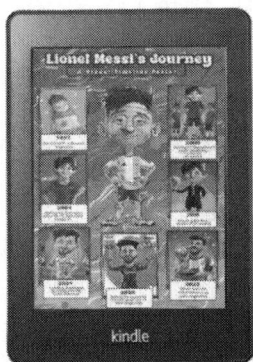

For instant access, go to:

www.sportsstoriesforkids.com/freegift

Please scan this QR code to access

www.sportsstoriesforkids.com/freegift

Table of Contents

Introduction

"Hey, why don't we go join them?"

Tommy nudged Sarah as he said this and pointed to the field where the other kids in their school were practicing soccer. It was a warm, sunny day, and they both loved playing soccer more than anything else in the whole world.

But Sarah hesitated. She bit her lip and looked down at her feet.

"I don't know, Tommy," she said quietly. "What if I'm not good enough? What if I mess up and let everyone down?"

Tommy frowned, sensing Sarah's fear. "But Sarah, you're amazing at soccer! Remember when you scored that goal last week? You were awesome!"

Sarah sighed, but her worries didn't go away. "I know, Tommy. But what if I get hurt? What if I'm not as good as everyone expects me to be?"

Tommy put his arm around Sarah's shoulder. "I understand, Sarah. But you know what? Everyone feels scared sometimes. Even the best soccer players in the world are sometimes scared of failing. But they don't let that stop them. They keep practicing and trying their best, no matter what."

Sarah looked up at Tommy, her eyes wide with hope. "Do you really think so, Tommy?"

Tommy smiled reassuringly. "Absolutely, Sarah! But before we play, let's take a moment to talk about some of the best soccer players in history and learn their stories. It can help us feel more confident and express ourselves better. Plus, it'll make us feel like we belong, and strengthen our friendship even more."

Sarah's eyes lit up with excitement. "That sounds awesome, Tommy! Who should we talk about first?"

Tommy thought for a moment before replying, "Well, how about we start with Lionel Messi? He's considered one of the greatest soccer players of all time. Did you know that he faced challenges too, just like us, but he never gave up? And look where he is now!"

As they discussed Messi's journey and the obstacles he overcame, Sarah felt inspired. She realized that even the best players have their doubts and fears, but they don't let them hold them back.

After talking about Messi, Tommy and Sarah delved into the stories of other legendary players like Cristiano Ronaldo, Mia Hamm, and Pele. With each story, they gained more confidence in themselves and their abilities.

By the time they finished, Sarah felt a newfound sense of determination. "Thanks, Tommy," she said, beaming. "I feel ready to take on anything now!"

Tommy grinned. "That's the spirit, Sarah! Now let's go out there and show everyone what we're made of!"

With their newfound confidence and strengthened friendship, Tommy and Sarah stepped onto the field, ready to play their hearts out and chase their dreams.

Have you ever felt like Sarah? You know, when you're super excited to play soccer, but then suddenly you start feeling scared? Well, guess what? There are lots of kids out there who feel the same way!

Sometimes we worry about not being good enough or letting our team down. And hey, getting hurt on the field is something that can make us nervous too. Plus, there's the pressure of living up to everyone's expectations, like our parents, coaches, or even ourselves.

But you know what? We're not alone! There are so many other kids who have the same fears and worries. And guess what else? There are ways to help us feel better and more confident!

Fortunately, we can always learn from some of the coolest soccer players ever! They've faced challenges too, and you know what they did? They never gave up! They showed us that even when things get tough, we can keep going and chase our dreams.

And hey, finding role models we can relate to is super important, especially for you girls who love soccer. We want to see people who look like us and have been through the same stuff we're going through.

4

But you know what else helps? Having friends who believe in us and cheer us on! And hey, if we ever feel down about our soccer skills, it's okay to talk about it. We can share our frustrations and challenges with friends and family, and they'll be there to support us.

Sometimes soccer can be tough, and we might have to deal with unfair play or mean teammates. But you know what? We can stand up for ourselves and each other! We can show good sportsmanship and always do our best, no matter what.

So, what are you waiting for?

Inspirational Short Soccer Stories for Kids will dive deep into the training regimens, game-winning strategies, and mental toughness routines used by world-class soccer players to dominate the field. You'll learn how soccer legends faced setbacks head-on, bounced back from adversity, and soared to the top of their game. Discover the resilience, determination, and unwavering spirit that propelled them to greatness. You also get to unleash your inner champion as you immerse yourself in the incredible stories, inspirational quotes, and jaw-dropping goals of these soccer heroes. Get fired up, get motivated, and get ready to take your game to the next level with the wisdom and guidance of the champions.

So yeah, soccer might have its challenges, but we're not giving up! We're gonna keep playing, keep learning, and keep having fun! Because at the end of the day, soccer is all about passion, friendship, and never giving up on our dreams! Let's do this, team!

CHAPTER 1

ALEX MORGAN

"Dream big, because dreams do happen."

-Alex Morgan

Who is Alex Morgan?

Alex Morgan is the coolest soccer player ever! Alex was born on July 2, 1989, in San Dimas, California. Alex became the youngest member of the US women's national soccer team in 2009 when she was just a teenager! How cool is that? And then, in 2011, she got to play in the FIFA World Cup! That's like the Superbowl of soccer, but for the whole world!

But wait, it gets even better! In 2012, at the Summer Olympic Games in London, Alex won her very first Olympic gold medal with the American team! Can you imagine standing on that podium, with a shiny gold medal around your neck? So epic!

But that's not all! In 2015, Alex achieved her big dream of winning a World Cup trophy! It was like the best day ever for soccer fans everywhere! And get this, the game she played in became the most-watched soccer match in US history!

Amazingly, Alex still plays soccer like a boss today! She's on the Orlando Pride team, showing everyone that girls can totally kick butt on the soccer field!

So yeah, that's Alex Morgan for you, a soccer superstar who's scored goals, won medals, and inspired kids like us all around the world! She's proof that if you work hard and follow your dreams, anything is possible!

More Than Just Goals

Alex Morgan is not just an amazing soccer player, she's also a total leader on and off the field!

First, Alex is super supportive of her teammates. Like, whenever someone scores a goal, she's the first one cheering them on and giving high-fives. She knows that soccer is a team sport, and she's always there to lift her teammates up and celebrate their successes.

But it's not just about the good times. Alex is also there for her team when things get tough. Like, if someone misses a shot or makes a mistake, she's quick to encourage them and remind them that they've got it. She's like the ultimate cheerleader, always motivating her teammates to keep going and never give up.

But Alex doesn't just talk the talk, she walks the walk. She's always leading by example. During the FIFA Women's World Cup 2019, Alex Morgan led USWNT - both in goals scored and in her vocal support. In the final match against the Netherlands, she scored a crucial goal, demonstrating her ability to perform under pressure and lead her team to victory. This shows young girls that they can be strong, powerful, and successful in whatever they do. Whether she's scoring goals on the field or speaking out for equality off the field, Alex Morgan is a true leader in every sense of the word.

Rising Above Challenges

Alex Morgan had always been a force on the soccer field, her speed and skill making her a standout player from a young age. But early in her career, she faced a serious challenge that threatened to derail her dreams.

On a sunny afternoon during high school, Alex went in for a tackle, only to feel a sharp pain shoot through her knee.

"Ouch! That really hurt," Alex winced as she fell to the ground, clutching her knee.

Her teammate rushed over. "Are you okay, Alex?"

Alex forced a smile. "I think so, but my knee really hurts."

At first, Alex was really scared. She tore her ACL and couldn't play soccer anymore, and that made her really sad. But instead of giving up, Alex decided to be super brave and work really hard to get better.

"Hey, Alex, you're going to get through this. We're all here for you," her teammate said, giving her a reassuring hug.

Every day, Alex did exercises to make her knee stronger. Sometimes it hurt, and she felt frustrated, but she never gave up. She knew that if she kept trying, she would get back to playing soccer again.

"This is really tough," Alex thought as she struggled with her exercises.

"You can do it, Alex! We believe in you," her teammates reassured her.

And you know what? Alex did it! After lots and lots of hard work, her knee was all better, and she could play soccer again. It was like a dream come true!

"I did it! I'm back!" Alex exclaimed, running onto the field with a huge grin on her face.

But the best part was how happy Alex was. She knew that even when things are tough, if you believe in yourself and never give up, you can do anything. And that's exactly what Alex did — she showed everyone that with a positive attitude and great determination, you can overcome any challenge!

Finding Your Voice

Alex Morgan isn't just a soccer superstar; she's also a real-life superhero for women's rights and pay equality. Whenever she's not scoring goals on the field, she's using her voice to make the world a better place for girls everywhere.

During one big interview in 2019, Alex was asked about pay equality for female athletes. Without hesitation, she spoke up loud and clear.

"I believe that girls and boys should be paid the same for doing the same job, whether it's playing soccer or anything else," she said with passion. She knew that girls deserve the same opportunities as boys, and she was determined to make sure they get them.

So, Alex Morgan and several of her teammates filed a gender discrimination lawsuit against the U.S. Soccer Federation, highlighting the big differences in pay and working conditions between the men's and women's national teams.

Her words spread like wildfire, inspiring young athletes all over the world to stand up for what they believe in. Their courage to take a stand started important conversations about gender equality in athletics. In schools and soccer fields everywhere, kids began to speak out about pay equality and women's rights. They held rallies, wrote letters to their leaders, and even started their own clubs to support each other.

And through it all, Alex Morgan was cheering them on. She knew that her platform as a famous athlete gave her the power to make a difference, and she wasn't afraid to use it.

Thanks to Alex and the countless young athletes she inspired, the world started to change. Girls everywhere began to see that they were worth just as much as boys – on the field, in the classroom, and everywhere else.

And as for Alex, she continues to score goals, break records, and fight for what she believes in. Because she knew that with a little bit of courage and great determination, anything is possible – on and off the soccer field.

Alex Morgan Reflection Questions

1. What do you think makes Alex Morgan a superhero on and off the soccer field? How can her story inspire you when things get tough?

2. Why do you think it's cool that Alex Morgan uses her voice to stand up for what she believes in? How can you use your voice to make a difference too?

3. How can you be brave and never give up, just like Alex Morgan did when she worked hard to overcome her knee injury?

CHAPTER 2

MEGAN RAPINOE

"We're gracious and we're humble, and we play the game a certain way, whether we win or lose."

-Megan Rapinoe

Who is Megan Rapinoe?

Wow, let me tell you about Megan Rapinoe! She's like the real-life superhero of soccer! Megan was born on July 5, 1985, in Redding, California, and from a young age, she was kicking soccer balls like nobody's business.

Fast forward to 2015, and Megan was on fire! She helped lead the United States Women's National Soccer Team to victory in the FIFA Women's World Cup, scoring some incredible goals along the way. But wait, there's more! In 2019, she did it again! Megan played a crucial role in securing another World Cup win for Team USA, proving that she's not just a soccer star, she's a soccer legend!

But Megan isn't just amazing on the field. In 2016, she took a stand by kneeling during the national anthem to protest racial inequality. Talk about bravery!

And get this, in 2021, Megan was awarded the Presidential Medal of Freedom for her incredible work on and off the soccer field. Can you believe it? She's not just a soccer hero; she's a real-life superhero!

Megan Rapinoe is more than just a soccer player; she's an inspiration to kids everywhere. She shows us that with hard work, determination, and dedication, we can achieve anything we set our minds to. Go, Megan, go!

A Double Threat

Megan Rapinoe isn't just a soccer player; she's a trailblazer. Let's dive into how she's using her platform to make a difference!

In 2016, during a National Women's Soccer League (NWSL) game, Megan took a knee during the national anthem to protest racial injustice, following in the footsteps of NFL quarterback Colin Kaepernick. This bold move sparked conversations across the nation about race, privilege, and activism in sports.

Then, in 2019, Megan made headlines again during the FIFA Women's World Cup. Not only did she lead the U.S. Women's National Team to victory with her exceptional skills, but she also used the spotlight to advocate for gender pay equality. During the tournament, she famously declared, "I'm not going to the (bad word alert!) White House," in response to President Trump's criticism of her and her teammates. This statement drew attention to the pay disparity between male and female athletes and amplified the ongoing fight for equal pay in sports.

What's more, in 2020, when lots of people were speaking up for fairness and equality, Megan was right there with them. She used her voice to speak out against unfair treatment of Black people. Together with other athletes, she asked for big changes to make things fair for everyone. Megan even asked the soccer community to stand up against unfair treatment, too.

Furthermore, Megan has been a vocal advocate for LGBTQ rights throughout her career. In 2019, she became the first openly gay woman to pose for the Sports Illustrated Swimsuit Issue, using the platform to promote visibility and acceptance for the LGBTQ community in sports.

Through her actions and words, Megan Rapinoe has shown that athletes have the power to drive meaningful change in society. She's not just scoring goals; she's scoring victories for social justice and equality.

Believing in Yourself

The sun beat down on the soccer field as Megan Rapinoe dribbled the ball with determination, her twin sister Rachael by her side. Their laughter echoed across the grass as they practiced their moves, their love for the game evident in every kick.

But as Megan grew older, doubts began to creep in. During a high school practice, her coach pulled her aside with a stern expression.

"Rapinoe, you've got talent, but you need to focus more," he said.

Megan's heart sank.

Was she not good enough?

Did she not belong on the field?

Despite her doubts, Megan refused to give up on her passion. She joined a local club team and poured her heart into every practice and game, determined to prove herself.

It wasn't until college that Megan truly found her stride. Playing for the University of Portland, she embraced her individuality and honed her skills on the field.

During her junior year, Megan faced a big moment. The team was down by one goal in the NCAA championship game. With only minutes left on the clock, Megan seized the opportunity and scored the equalizing goal, leading her team to victory in overtime.

From that moment on, Megan's confidence soared. She knew she had what it took to compete at the highest level, and she was determined to make her mark on the world of soccer.

After college, Megan joined the U.S. Women's National Team and quickly made a name for herself as a fierce competitor.

The Power of Conviction

Megan Rapinoe had always been told to stay quiet, to keep her head down and focus on the game. But deep inside, she knew she couldn't stay silent. She had a fire burning within her, a passion for justice that couldn't be extinguished.

She wasn't afraid to speak up, even when it was tough.

"Hey Megan, why do you always have to talk about stuff other than soccer?" her teammate asked.

"Because there are important things that need to be said," Megan replied. "Like how everyone should be treated fairly, no matter who they are."

Even though some people didn't like it, Megan kept using her voice to stand up for what she believed in.

"You know, Meg, you're going to get in trouble if you keep doing this," her coach warned.

"I know, but I can't just stay quiet when I see things that aren't right," Megan said.

In 2019, Megan led her team to win the World Cup. It was a big deal, not just for soccer, but as proof that everyone deserves a fair shot.

"We did it!" Megan shouted after the win. "And we're not done yet. There's still so much more to do."

Off the field, Megan kept fighting for equality.

"Why do you care so much about this stuff?" her friend asked.

"Because it's important," Megan replied. "And because I want to make the world a better place for everyone."

Through it all, Megan learned that being true to herself was the most important thing.

"I may not always fit in, but that's okay." she said. "As long as I'm standing up for what's right, that's all that matters."

Megan Rapinoe Reflection Questions

1. How do you think Megan Rapinoe felt when she faced criticism for speaking up about important issues?

2. Why do you think Megan Rapinoe believes it's important to use her voice to stand up for equality and fairness?

3. What can we learn from Megan Rapinoe about being true to ourselves and standing up for what we believe in, even when it's difficult?

CHAPTER 3

LIONEL MESSI

"There are more important things in life than winning or losing a game."

-*Lionel Messi*

Who is Lionel Messi?

Oh my gosh, you won't believe how amazing Lionel Messi's life is! So, get this, his full name is Luis Lionel Andres Messi, and he was born on June 24, 1987, in Rosario, Argentina. Can you imagine being born in the same year as him?

Okay, so when Messi was just a little kid, he was diagnosed with growth hormone deficiency, which meant he was smaller than other kids his age. But guess what? That didn't stop him! His parents couldn't afford his treatment at first, but then something incredible happened.

In 2000, when Messi was only 13 years old, his family arranged a trial for him with FC Barcelona, one of the best soccer clubs in the world! And they were so impressed with him that they signed him right away! Can you imagine signing a contract with one of the biggest clubs in the world when you're only 13? It's a dream come true!

But wait, it gets even better. Messi made his debut for Barcelona's senior team when he was just 17 years old! And he became the youngest player ever to score for the club! Isn't that incredible?

And you know what's even more amazing? Messi has won so many awards and broken so many records! He's won the Ballon d'Or award SEVEN times! Can you believe that? Seven times! He's like the king of soccer!

Oh, and Messi's scored over 700 goals in his career! That's more goals than I can even imagine! And he's broken so many records along the way, like becoming Barcelona's all-time leading goal scorer and the youngest player to score 100 goals in the UEFA Champions League! It's like he's breaking records every time he steps onto the field!

But you know what's the best part? Messi's not just an amazing soccer player, he's also a really great person. He's always giving back to his community and helping kids who are less fortunate. Isn't that awesome?

So yeah, Lionel Messi's life is basically a fairy tale come to life. He's overcome so many challenges, achieved so much, and he's just getting started! I can't wait to see what he does next!

The Maestro of the Ball

Imagine Lionel Messi on the soccer field, dribbling the ball like a wizard! But how does he do it? Well, let's uncover the secrets behind Messi's magical ball control!

First, Messi has this cool thing called a low center of gravity. Because he's closer to the ground, this helps him stay super balanced and nimble. That means he can twist and turn without losing his footing, leaving defenders scratching their heads!

Next, Messi's got some serious skills when it comes to keeping the ball close to his feet. It's like the ball is stuck to him with magic! He practices dribbling drills all the time, where he taps the ball really fast and moves it around with pinpoint precision.

Did you know that Messi also has amazing body control? He knows exactly how to use his body to shield the ball from defenders while he zooms past them. It's like he's dancing with the ball, and the defenders can't keep up!

But wait, there's more! Messi has this superpower called vision and awareness. He sees the whole soccer field like a puzzle, knowing where everyone is and how to sneak past them. It's like he has eyes in the back of his head!

And he never stops practicing. He's always out there on the field, dribbling through cones and dodging imaginary defenders. He's like a superhero training to save the day!

So, there you have it! Messi's magical ball control is a mix of natural talent, lots of practice, and a sprinkle of soccer genius. He's not just a soccer player – he's a dribbling wizard!

From Scrawny to Superstar

When Lionel Messi was a kid, he faced a big challenge. He wasn't growing like other kids his age because of a growth hormone deficiency.

"Mom, why am I so small?" Messi asked one day, looking up at his worried mother.

His parents, Jorge and Celia, were concerned. They knew they had to find a way to help him.

"We'll figure it out, Leo," his father reassured him, his voice filled with determination.

Despite their financial struggles, Messi's parents never lost hope. They searched for ways to afford his treatment, which cost $900 a month.

"We'll find a solution, Leo. Don't worry," his mother said, her eyes filled with determination.

One day, Messi's father learned about a trial with Barcelona, a famous soccer club in Spain.

"Leo, Barcelona wants to see you play!" his father exclaimed, his voice tinged with excitement.

Messi couldn't believe it. Barcelona was a dream come true for any soccer player.

"Really, Dad? Barcelona?" he asked, his eyes wide with excitement.

After a successful trial, Barcelona offered Messi a chance to join their youth team. "Leo, you did it! You're going to play for Barcelona!" his father said, his voice filled with pride.

Messi's journey to greatness wasn't easy, but he never gave up. With hard work and determination, he overcame his obstacles and became one of the greatest soccer players of all time. "I'm proud of you, Leo," his father said, tears of joy in his eyes.

And Messi smiled, knowing that anything was possible if he believed in himself.

Dedication that Defines Him

Lionel Messi is not just a soccer superstar; he's also a hero off the field. He's been involved in projects to help kids around the world, like building schools, providing healthcare, and fun activities. Since 2020, Messi has been working with organizations like UNICEF and the Lionel Messi Foundation to make a positive impact on children's lives.

But Messi's greatness doesn't stop there. He's always striving to improve his game. Since he was a young boy growing up in Rosario, Argentina, he's practiced new skills and techniques every day. From 2000, when he joined Barcelona's youth academy, until now, Messi has dedicated countless hours to training and perfecting his craft.

When he's not on the field, Messi cherishes time with his family. Since 2008, he's been in a relationship with Antonella Roccuzzo, his childhood friend's cousin. They have three sons together, Thiago, Mateo, and Ciro, born in 2012, 2015, and 2018 respectively. Messi knows the importance of balancing his career with family time, showing that being successful means more than just winning games.

So, whether he's scoring goals or making a difference in the world, Lionel Messi continues to inspire and lead by example, showing kids everywhere that with hard work, dedication, and kindness, anything is possible.

Lionel Messi Reflection Questions

1. What do you think makes Lionel Messi such a good soccer player? Do you practice any of the same skills he does?

2. How does Lionel Messi help other kids around the world? Why do you think it's important for famous people to help others?

3. If you could meet Lionel Messi, what would you ask him? What do you think you could learn from him?

CHAPTER 4

CRISTIANO RONALDO

"I'm living a dream I never want to wake up from."

-Cristiano Ronaldo

Who is Cristiano Ronaldo?

Let's dive into the amazing life of Cristiano Ronaldo! Imagine, it all started on February 5, 1985, when Cristiano was born in Funchal, Madeira, Portugal. When he was just a little kid, his dad, José Dinis Aveiro, was a kit man at a local soccer club, and Cristiano caught the soccer bug from him.

At the age of 8, Ronaldo began playing for Andorinha, his dad's club, showing off his incredible skills. But it wasn't until he was 12 that he moved to the mainland to join the Sporting CP youth academy. That's where he really honed his talent and caught the eye of soccer scouts.

In 2003, when he was 18 years old, Ronaldo signed with Manchester United, one of the biggest clubs in England. Can you believe it? Just five years later, in 2008, he helped Manchester United win the Champions League!

But Ronaldo's journey didn't stop there. In 2009, he made a big move to Real Madrid with a transfer fee of £80 million, becoming the most expensive soccer player in the world at the time. At Real Madrid, he won four Champions League titles and became one of the greatest players of all time!

In 2018, Ronaldo joined Juventus, a top Italian club, where he continued to show off his amazing skills and won two Serie A titles. And guess what? He even returned to Manchester United in 2021, where it all began for him in England!

But it's not just about soccer for Ronaldo. He's also a successful businessman with his own line of CR7-branded products, including clothing and fragrances. Plus, he's a big-hearted guy, involved in lots of charity work to help kids in need.

And get this, in 2017, the Madeira International Airport in Portugal was renamed Cristiano Ronaldo International Airport! Can you imagine having an airport named after you? That's how famous and awesome Cristiano Ronaldo is!

So, there you have it, the incredible life of Cristiano Ronaldo, from a little kid with big dreams to one of the greatest soccer players and role models in the world!

Machine Made for Goals

Even as a little kid, Ronaldo's passion for the game was HUGE! He would practice day in and day out, chasing his dream of becoming the best soccer player in the world. And guess what? His hard work paid off big time!

One sunny day, Cristiano and his friends were playing soccer in the park. Cristiano dribbled the ball with fancy footwork, showing off his skills. His friend Miguel said, "Wow, Cristiano, you're amazing! How do you get so good at soccer?"

Cristiano grinned and replied, "I practice every day! Even when it's raining, I'm out here kicking the ball around."

Pedro, another friend, chimed in, "But don't you ever get tired?"

Cristiano shook his head. "Nah, I love it too much! My dream is to be the best soccer player in the world!"

As the years went by, Cristiano's love for soccer only grew stronger. He trained harder than anyone else, running laps, practicing his kicks, and never giving up.

His mom would often call him in for dinner, but Cristiano would say, "Just one more goal, Mom! I'm almost there!"

One day, a coach from a big soccer club came to watch Cristiano play. He was amazed by Cristiano's skills and offered him a spot on the team. Cristiano's eyes lit up with excitement. "This is it, guys! My big break!"

From that day on, Cristiano worked even harder. He woke up early, ate a healthy breakfast, and trained with all his might. His coach would say, "Cristiano, you're like a machine! How do you keep going?"

Cristiano would just smile and reply, "It's my passion, coach! I'll do whatever it takes to reach my goal!"

And reach his goal he did! Cristiano became one of the best soccer players in the world, scoring goals and winning trophies wherever he went. But no matter how famous he became, Cristiano never forgot where he came from or how hard he had worked to get there.

So, kids, remember Cristiano's story the next time you're out playing soccer. With dedication, hard work, and a little bit of magic, you can achieve anything you set your mind to!

The Art of Reinvention

No matter what, Cristiano Ronaldo keeps improving his playing style to make sure he remains at the top. He knows that times change, so he changes with them! He does this by pushing himself every day on the field.

It all started in 2003. Ronaldo had to learn from Sir Alex Ferguson, and he challenged himself by refining his technique and understanding of the game. Later on, when he moved on to Real Madrid, Ronaldo moved on to using a more central attack playing style. He focused everything on scoring goals and being a clinical finisher!

But, it's not just about Ronaldo's changing styles. It's also about how he makes sure he is always in top shape. He is always improving his strength, speed, and agility. Now, he is at his peak performance well into his thirties!

Along with all of this, Ronaldo has mastered various goal-scoring techniques over the years. These were all about powerful long-range shots, headers, and precise finishing inside the box. He consistently is thinking about his own skills and how to make them even better.

Even as soccer changed over time, Ronaldo kept adapting to different systems and playing styles. Whether deployed as a winger, striker, or attacking midfielder, he uses his brain to do his best, no matter the job.

Even as he is getting older, Ronaldo is always looking for excellence. Whether he is breaking records, winning titles, or inspiring the next generation of soccer players, he continues to push the boundaries of what is achievable, leaving a bright mark on the sport.

Cristiano Ronaldo Reflection Questions

1. What do you think makes Cristiano Ronaldo so good at playing soccer?

2. If you could meet Cristiano Ronaldo, what would you ask him about soccer?

3. How does Cristiano Ronaldo inspire you to work hard and follow your dreams, on or off the soccer field?

CHAPTER 5

KYLIAN MBAPPÉ

"I am happy, and I am living the life I always dreamed of."

-Kylian Mbappe

Who is Kylian Mbappé?

Let me tell you about Kylian Mbappé - he's like a soccer superhero! Kylian was born on December 20, 1998, right in the heart of Paris, France. Can you imagine growing up in such an amazing city? Well, Kylian did, and he's been kicking a soccer ball around since he was just a little kid!

Kylian's parents, Fayza and Wilfried, must have known from the start that their son had something special. You see, his dad was a coach for a local club called AS Bondy, and that's where Kylian got his first taste of soccer. He was like a lightning bolt on the field, zooming past everyone with his incredible speed.

But Kylian didn't stop there. At 14 years old, he signed with AS Monaco, one of the big soccer clubs in France. Can you imagine being a professional soccer player at that age? It's like a dream come true!

Then, on December 2, 2015, something amazing happened - Kylian made his debut for AS Monaco's first team. And get this, he was only 17 years old! That's super young to play with the big boys, but Kylian wasn't afraid. He showed everyone what he was made of, scoring goals and making fans go wild!

But Kylian's journey didn't stop with Monaco. In August 2017, he joined Paris Saint-Germain (PSG), another top club in France. And let me tell you, he became a real superstar there. With his lightning-fast moves and incredible goal-scoring skills, Kylian led PSG to victory after victory.

And Kylian's not just a star in France - he's also a hero for his country. He made his debut for the French national team in 2017, and since then, he's been dazzling fans all over the world. He even helped France win the FIFA World Cup in 2018! Can you imagine lifting the biggest trophy in soccer at just 19 years old? It's like something out of a movie!

Kylian's journey from a kid kicking a ball around in Paris to one of the greatest soccer players in the world is truly inspiring. And who knows what amazing things he'll do next? One thing's for sure - wherever Kylian goes, he'll keep thrilling fans and showing the world what he's made of!

Blazing Speed, Blazing Future

"Kylian, I gotta tell you, I'm super proud of you!" Kylian's Dad, Wilfried, exclaimed, patting Kylian's shoulder.

Kylian sat in the locker room, buzzing with excitement for the upcoming match. He beamed up at his dad, his eyes shining with excitement. "Thanks, Dad! It's been so awesome!"

Wilfried's admiration was written all over his face. "You've worked crazy hard for this, buddy. Being the youngest player on AS Monaco's first team is huge!"

Kylian's grin widened, feeling like he was on top of the world. "Yeah, it's like a dream come true, Dad. I've always wanted to play at this level!"

Wilfried chuckled, remembering their days kicking the ball around in the park. "I remember when you were just a little guy, running around with that soccer ball. But now, you're living the dream!"

Kylian nodded eagerly, still feeling the rush of the game.

"It's all happening so fast, Dad! But I'm ready! I wanna be the best player out there!"

Wilfried gave Kylian's shoulder a gentle squeeze. "I know you will be, Kylian. Just keep working hard, stay focused, and never forget where you came from."

Kylian's determination shone through as he nodded back. "Thanks, Dad! I won't let you down!"

As they sat together, excitement filled the air, both father and son looking forward to the amazing adventures ahead. But then, Wilfried's tone turned serious.

"You know, Kylian, this is gonna be way tougher than those days when we played together. I'm the coach and director for AS Bondy, where you started playing at six years old. This is the big leagues now, buddy. Are you gonna be ready?"

Kylian's eyes widened, a mixture of excitement and determination flooding through him.

"You bet, Dad! I'm gonna give it everything I've got! I'm ready for the challenge!"

Sure enough, Kylian went on to prove himself on the field, just as he promised his dad. It was a crisp autumn afternoon, and the stadium was buzzing with anticipation as Kylian dashed onto the pitch.

As soon as the referee blew the whistle, Kylian exploded into action, his lightning pace leaving defenders in the dust. With every swift movement, he weaved through the opposition's defense like a magician, his electrifying footwork mesmerizing the crowd.

With each touch of the ball, Kylian seemed to dance across the field, effortlessly gliding past defenders with his quick turns and sudden bursts of speed. His opponents could barely keep up, their attempts to stop him futile against his skill and agility.

With a flick of his foot, Kylian sent the ball soaring into the back of the net, the crowd erupting into cheers as they witnessed his brilliance once again. His performance on the field was nothing short of spectacular, a true testament to his incredible talent and dedication to the game.

As the final whistle blew, Kylian walked off the field with a satisfied smile, knowing that he had once again left his mark on the game. With his lightning pace and electrifying footwork, he had proven himself to be a nightmare for defenders everywhere, cementing his status as one of the greatest players of his generation.

But, the most exciting part about Mbappe's journey is what lies ahead! This story happened when he was only 17. Now in 2024, he's still only 25, and he's taking the world by storm! He's already accomplished more than most players could dream of in a lifetime. With his skill, determination, and hunger for success, there's no telling how far he can go. Whether it's winning more trophies, breaking more records, or earning his place as one of the all-time greats, one thing is for certain: the future is incredibly bright for Kylian Mbappé.

Learning from the Best

As a young boy, Kylian sat wide-eyed in front of the television, mesmerized by the breathtaking skills of Lionel Messi and Cristiano Ronaldo. With each flick of the ball and lightning-fast run down the field, he felt a surge of excitement and inspiration. Watching these soccer legends weave their magic on the pitch, Kylian couldn't help but dream big.

"I want to be like them one day," he whispered to himself, his gaze fixed on the screen. He imagined himself scoring goals like Messi, with precision and finesse, or dazzling defenders with skillful footwork like Ronaldo. The thought of playing at their level filled him with determination and ambition.

As the match went on before him, Kylian studied every move, absorbing every detail of their play. He knew that being great like Messi and Ronaldo wouldn't be easy, but he was willing to work hard and chase his dreams with unwavering dedication.

So, Kylian spent hours practicing in his backyard, trying to copy Ronaldo's tricks and kicks. He'd run around pretending to be Ronaldo, imagining he was playing in front of thousands of cheering fans.

Sometimes, Kylian's friends would join him, and they'd pretend to be a whole team of Ronaldos, scoring goals and celebrating just like their hero. They'd cheer each other on and dream about playing soccer professionally one day.

Even though Kylian was just a kid, he knew that if he practiced hard and never gave up, he could become a great soccer player, just like Cristiano Ronaldo. And every time he stepped onto the field, he'd remember the lessons he learned from his idol, ready to chase his dreams with all his heart.

As Kylian's career blossomed, he found himself training alongside Lionel Messi at Paris Saint-Germain. The opportunity to learn from one of the greatest players in the world was a dream come true for Kylian.

One day, during a training session, Messi approached Kylian with a friendly smile. "Hey, Kylian, I noticed something in your footwork. Can I show you a trick that might help?"

Kylian's eyes widened in excitement. "Of course, Messi! I'd love to learn from you."

Messi demonstrated a subtle shift in body positioning before executing a quick turn with the ball at his feet.

"It's all about using your body to deceive the defender," Messi explained. "Try it out."

Kylian nodded eagerly and attempted to replicate Messi's move. At first, he stumbled a bit, but with Messi's patient guidance, he soon started to get the hang of it.

"See, like that," Messi said with a nod of approval. "You've got the talent, Kylian. Keep practicing, and you'll master it in no time."

Kylian beamed with gratitude. "Thanks, Messi! I can't believe I'm learning from you. It's like a dream."

Messi chuckled. "Believe me, Kylian, dreams can come true with hard work and dedication. Just keep pushing yourself, and you'll achieve great things."

From that day on, Kylian soaked up every bit of advice and wisdom Messi shared with him. Their training sessions became not only a chance to improve his skills but also an opportunity to forge a bond with his idol, propelling him closer to his own path of greatness.

As you can see, Kylian Mbappé embraces every opportunity to learn from the greats. Whether it's studying Cristiano Ronaldo's moves or training alongside Lionel Messi, he understands the value of soaking up knowledge from those who have paved the way for soccer greatness. With a humble heart and a hunger for improvement, Kylian continues to push himself to new heights, unafraid to seek guidance and wisdom from soccer legends. In doing so, he not only hones his skills but also embodies the spirit of true sportsmanship and dedication to his craft.

Pressure Makes Diamonds

Imagine being in Kylian Mbappé's shoes when the whole world is watching, and the pressure is so intense you can feel it in every heartbeat. But instead of feeling scared or nervous, Kylian is like a superhero, ready to take on any challenge that comes his way. He doesn't back down; he faces it head-on with a smile on his face and fire in his eyes.

When it's time for the big game or the crucial moment, Kylian doesn't let the pressure get to him. He doesn't freeze up or second-guess himself. Instead, he thrives in those high-stake situations, using the energy and excitement to fuel his performance. He turns the pressure into rocket fuel, propelling himself to greatness.

Whether it's a penalty shootout in the World Cup final or a decisive match in the league, Kylian always rises to the occasion. He doesn't just play; he dominates. He doesn't just show up; he steals the show. That's what makes him more than a soccer player; he's a living legend in the making, rewriting the rules of the game with every goal he scores and every match he wins.

Kylian Mbappé Reflection Questions

1. Have you ever felt nervous before a big game or event? How do you think Kylian Mbappé deals with pressure and performs so well under it?

2. What do you think makes Kylian Mbappé such a successful soccer player? How does he use his skills and determination to achieve his goals?

3. If you could ask Kylian Mbappé one question about his journey to becoming a professional soccer player, what would it be? What could you learn from his experiences?

CHAPTER 6

NEYMAR

"I always dribble for a reason, and I always head for the goal."

-Neymar

Who is Neymar?

Neymar, oh my gosh, let me tell you about Neymar! He's like this soccer superhero from Brazil, born on February 5, 1992, in Mogi das Cruzes, São Paulo. Can you imagine? A real-life superhero! His full name is Neymar da Silva Santos Jr., but everyone just calls him Neymar.

So, get this, Neymar's dad used to be a soccer player too! From the time Neymar was a little kid, he was obsessed with soccer. He played street games and this indoor version called futsal. He was unstoppable, even back then.

Then, when he was 11 years old, he joined the youth team of Santos FC. That's a big deal in Brazil! It's where legends like Pelé started their careers. Can you imagine being 11 and joining a team like that? But Neymar wasn't just any kid; he was special.

Oh, and when Neymar was 14, Real Madrid, yeah, that Real Madrid, wanted him to come play for them! But you know what? Neymar said no! Can you believe it? He stayed with Santos because they promised him big things, and boy, did he deliver!

In 2009, Neymar made his professional debut for Santos FC, and from there, he was on fire! He won all these awards and helped Santos win championships. Then, in 2013, he joined FC Barcelona. You know, the team with Messi and all those other superstars? Neymar fit right in and helped them win everything!

But wait, it gets crazier! In 2017, Neymar moved to Paris Saint-Germain (PSG), and everyone was talking about it. He became one of the highest-paid players ever! And then, just when you think you've seen it all, in 2023, Neymar signed with Al-Hilal, a team in Saudi Arabia.

But Neymar isn't just famous for his soccer skills; he's also a big deal for Brazil! He's played for the national team since 2010, and he's scored so many goals! He's like a hero to everyone back home.

So yeah, that's Neymar for you! A soccer legend in the making, from playing in the streets to becoming one of the biggest names in the world!

The Samba Magician

Neymar's playing style is a symphony of skill and creativity, choreographed with the finesse of a master conductor. He's not just a soccer player; he's an artist on the field, painting breathtaking masterpieces with every touch of the ball.

One of Neymar's most mesmerizing traits is his dazzling dribbling ability. It's like he has the ball on a string, effortlessly weaving through defenders with swift changes of direction and lightning-quick footwork. His close control is second to none, leaving opponents grasping at thin air as he glides past them with ease.

But it's not just Neymar's dribbling that sets him apart; it's his flair for the unexpected. He's always one step ahead of the game, pulling off audacious tricks and flicks that defy belief. Whether it's a cheeky backheel pass or a gravity-defying sombrero flick, Neymar's creativity knows no bounds.

And let's not forget about his eye for goal. Neymar has a lethal combination of power and precision, capable of scoring from anywhere on the field. Whether it's a thunderous strike from outside the box or a delicate chip over the goalkeeper, he knows how to find the back of the net in style.

But perhaps what truly sets Neymar apart is his ability to entertain. He doesn't just play soccer; he puts on a show. From his signature step-overs to his celebratory dances, Neymar knows how to captivate an audience and leave them begging for more.

In the end, Neymar's playing style is more than just a collection of skills; it's a reflection of his personality. Bold, expressive, and always full of surprises, he brings a touch of magic to the beautiful game that will be remembered for generations to come.

The Comeback Kid

One time, during a big soccer game, Neymar got really hurt. He was playing for Brazil against Colombia in the World Cup. Neymar's back got hurt when a player from the other team crashed into him.

"Ouch! My back hurts!" Neymar cried out.

Concerned teammates rushed to his side as the referee blew the whistle to stop the play. Medical staff hurried onto the field, their faces etched with worry.

"It hurts so much," Neymar muttered through gritted teeth as they carefully examined him.

After a tense few moments, the medical team made a sad decision.

"It's serious, Neymar," one of them said sadly. "You've fractured your vertebrae. You'll have to be stretchered off."

Neymar's heart sank as the reality of the situation set in.

"But the World Cup... I can't miss it," he protested weakly.

"I'm sorry, Neymar," the doctor replied gently. "You won't be able to continue playing in this tournament."

As Neymar was carried off the field on a stretcher, the crowd fell silent, their cheers replaced by sad murmurs. It was a hard blow for Brazil, losing their star player in such a crucial match.

Despite the pain, Neymar remained determined to recover.

"I'll be back," he vowed to his teammates as they offered words of encouragement.

And true to his word, Neymar's hard work and determination saw him through the long road to recovery. Though he missed the rest of the tournament, his spirit was strong, and he was ready to return even better than ever.

The funny thing is, Neymar kept getting hurt.

Each time, he never gave up.

In 2018, he hurt his foot while playing for PSG. It was a serious injury, and he had to get surgery. Everyone thought he might not be able to play for a long time. But Neymar didn't give up. He worked hard to get better and make a comeback.

Then, in 2020, during a big match, Neymar hurt his ankle. At first, it seemed really bad, and people were worried. But Neymar didn't let it get him down. He rested, worked with the doctors, and before long, he was back on the field, showing off his skills once again.

In 2021, Neymar faced another challenge. He got a groin injury during a game. It was frustrating for him because he had to sit out for a few weeks while his team played on without him. But Neymar didn't lose hope. He stayed positive and focused on getting better.

And then, in 2023, just when Neymar thought he was in top form, illness struck. He had to miss a game because he was sick. But Neymar didn't let it bring him down. He knew he would bounce back, just like he always did.

Through all these tough times, Neymar never gave up. He showed that with determination and hard work, you can overcome any obstacle. And each time he got knocked down, he got right back up, ready to conquer the soccer world once again.

Neymar Reflection Questions

1. Looking at Neymar's career, what do you think are some of the biggest challenges he faced? How did he overcome them?

2. What do you think motivates Neymar to keep pushing forward despite setbacks and injuries? How does his determination inspire you in your own life?

3. Reflecting on Neymar's journey from his early days to becoming a global soccer superstar, what lessons can you learn from these two big words: *resilience* and *perseverance*?

CHAPTER 7

PELÉ

"Everything is Practice."

-*Pele*

Who is Pelé?

Pelé was born on October 23, 1940, in Três Corações, Brazil. Pelé wasn't always a soccer superstar. When he was a little kid, he used to play street soccer barefoot because his family didn't have much money. But guess what? That didn't stop him from becoming one of the greatest soccer players of all time!

When Pelé was 17 years old, he made his debut for the Brazilian national team. Can you believe it? He was already playing with the big kids! And he didn't just play – he totally rocked it! In 1958, at the young age of 17, Pelé helped Brazil win their first-ever World Cup championship. That's the biggest trophy in the world of soccer!

But Pelé didn't stop there. Nope, he kept on scoring goals and making awesome plays. In 1962, he tore a muscle in his leg during the World Cup, but that didn't hold him back. Brazil still won the tournament, and Pelé showed everyone that he was a true champion.

Then, in 1970, Pelé did it again! He led Brazil to their third World Cup victory, and he even scored in the final game. Talk about a soccer legend!

But wait, there's more! Pelé wasn't just amazing on the field – he was also a super nice guy off the field. He used his fame to help promote peace and bring people together through soccer. In fact, he even won the International Peace Award in 1978. How cool is that?

So, that's the story of Pelé … the barefoot boy who became a soccer superstar and inspired millions of people around the world.

The King of Soccer

In the annals of soccer history, Pelé stands tall as one of the greatest players to ever grace the pitch. His name reverberates through the ages, synonymous with skill, finesse, and an unparalleled ability to find the back of the net. As the sun set on his illustrious career, the world paused to reflect on the legacy he had etched into the beautiful game.

"It's Pelé!" The commentator's voice echoed across the stadium as the young Brazilian maestro dazzled spectators with his mesmerizing footwork. From the favelas of Brazil to the grand stages of the World Cup, Pelé's journey was a testament to his sheer talent and unwavering determination.

"You have to believe in yourself," Pelé's father's voice echoed in his ears as he trained tirelessly, honing his skills in the dusty streets of Três Corações. With every kick of the ball, he harbored dreams of glory, dreams that would soon materialize on the grandest stage of all.

In the 1958 World Cup final, as the tension mounted and the world held its breath, Pelé unleashed a thunderous strike that rippled the back of the net. "Goooaaal!" erupted the crowd as Brazil clinched their first-ever World Cup title, and a star was born.

"You're a natural, Pelé," his teammates would often remark, in awe of his uncanny ability to find space and score seemingly impossible goals. With each tournament, Pelé continued to rewrite the record books, leaving defenders in his wake and goalkeepers clutching at thin air.

"It's not just about the goals," Pelé would humbly reply when asked about his incredible goalscoring record. "It's about the joy of playing the game and sharing that joy with others." And indeed, Pelé's impact transcended statistics; the joy he brought to millions of fans around the world truly set him apart.

At the end of his illustrious career, Pelé's legacy was secure. From his unparalleled goalscoring record to his dominance on the world stage, he had left an indelible mark on the beautiful game. And though he hung up his boots, his spirit continues to inspire generations of soccer players, ensuring that the legend of Pelé will live on for eternity.

A Master of the Beautiful Game

One day, as the team gathered for practice, a young teammate approached Pelé with a mixture of awe and admiration in his eyes.

"Wow, Pelé," he exclaimed, "how did you get so good at soccer?"

Pelé flashed a warm smile before gesturing for the young player to join him on the field. "Come, let me show you," he replied, his voice tinged with enthusiasm.

With patience and precision, Pelé began to impart his wealth of knowledge upon his eager pupil. He demonstrated exceptional dribbling skills, weaving effortlessly through imaginary defenders with grace and finesse. "It's all about control and confidence," Pelé explained, his movements fluid and precise.

Next, he showcased his powerful finishing ability, unleashing thunderous strikes that found the back of the net with unerring accuracy.

"Always keep your eye on the goal," Pelé advised, as the ball soared into the top corner with breathtaking speed.

But perhaps most importantly, Pelé emphasized the importance of vision and creativity on the field. With a flick of his foot, he orchestrated intricate passing sequences, creating scoring opportunities for his teammates with effortless ease.

"Soccer is a team sport," Pelé reminded his pupil, "and it's up to each of us to play our part."

As the sun dipped below the horizon and the practice came to an end, the young player thanked Pelé for his invaluable lessons. "I'll never forget this," he said, his eyes shining with newfound determination. And as they walked off the field together, Pelé couldn't help but feel a sense of pride, knowing that he had passed on his passion for the game to the next generation of soccer stars.

Beyond the Pitch

One sunny afternoon in the 1960's, Pelé was walking through the streets of his town when he noticed something troubling. People were treated unfairly because of the color of their skin. This made Pelé very sad.

"Daddy, why are those people being treated differently?" asked a young girl, tugging at her father's sleeve as they passed by.

Pelé paused, then knelt down to her level.

"It's not right, sweetheart," he said gently. "Everyone deserves to be treated with kindness and respect, no matter what they look like."

Determined to make a difference, Pelé decided to use his voice to speak out against racial discrimination. He joined marches and protests, where people from all walks of life came together to demand equality and justice.

During one of these events, Pelé stood tall and spoke passionately about the importance of treating everyone with kindness and respect, no matter their race or background. "We must stand together," he declared, his voice ringing out strong and clear.

"You're right, Pelé," said a man in the crowd, nodding in agreement. "We can't let injustice continue. Together, we can make a difference."

Pelé smiled, grateful for the support. "That's the spirit," he said. "Together, we can change the world."

After making a big difference during the Civil Rights Movement, Pelé didn't stop there!

Pelé often attended big events where people from different countries came together to talk about friendship and collaboration. He talked about how important it was for everyone to be kind and help each other, no matter where they come from.

He also liked to help people in need. Pelé would go to places where there wasn't a lot of money or food and try to make things better. He did things like playing in charity games or visiting sick kids in the hospital. He wanted to make sure everyone had a chance to be happy and healthy.

Pelé really cared about kids, too! He wanted to help them reach their dreams, especially if they didn't have a lot of money or resources. He would go to schools and sports clubs to talk to kids about chasing their dreams and never giving up, even when things got tough.

And even when Pelé got older, he still liked to be part of events where people would give him awards and throw parties to say thank you for everything he did to make the world a better place.

Pelé's kindness and big heart inspired people all around the world. He showed that anyone could make a difference, big or small. And that's why he'll always be remembered as a true champion, on and off the soccer field!

Pelé Reflection Questions

1. How do you think Pelé's experiences during the Civil Rights Movement shaped his beliefs about fairness and equality?

2. Why do you think Pelé is often considered one of the greatest soccer players of all time?

3. How did Pelé's soccer career influence the way people view the sport today?

CHAPTER 8

MIA HAMM

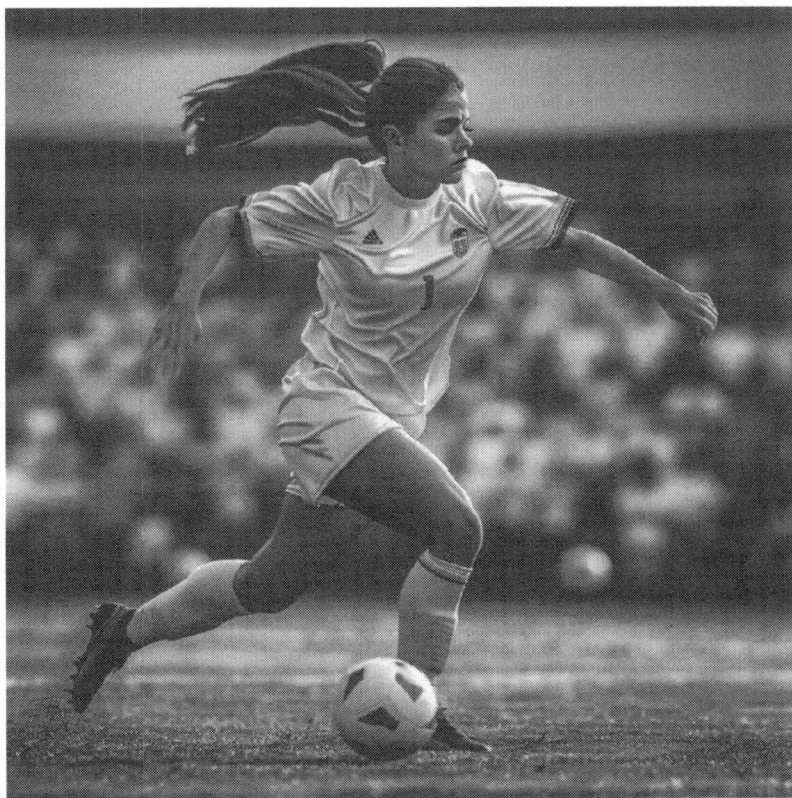

"I am building a fire, and every day I train, I add more fuel. At just the right moment, I light the match."

-Mia Hamm

Who is Mia Hamm?

Oh my gosh, let me tell you all about Mia Hamm! Mia Hamm was born on March 17, 1972, in Selma, Alabama. She grew up in a big family with six kids! She was the fourth oldest. Her dad was in the Air Force, so they moved around a lot. This made her a "military brat," and she got to live in lots of different places.

When Mia was 8, her parents adopted her brother Garrett, who she really looked up to. He was one of her heroes! Sadly, Garrett passed away in 1997 from a rare bone marrow disease, and that was really hard for her.

Mia got married to her college sweetheart, Christian Corry, in 1994, but they later divorced. Then, in 2003, she married Nomar Garciaparra, a famous baseball player. They have three kids together: twin girls Grace and Ava, born in 2007, and a son named Garrett, born in 2012, named after her late brother.

Mia was a soccer superstar from a young age! She joined the U.S. Women's National Soccer Team in 1987, when she was just 15 years old. She played forward and was amazing at scoring goals. In 1991, Mia helped the U.S. team win their first-ever Women's World Cup! It was a huge deal!

Then in 1996, she played in the Olympics in Atlanta and helped the team win the gold medal. This was the first time women's soccer was in the Olympics, and they won! In 1999, the U.S. team won the Women's World Cup again, and it was super exciting. The final game was held in Pasadena, California, and Mia and her team played in front of over 90,000 fans!

In 2004, she won another gold medal in the Athens Olympics and then retired from professional soccer. By the time she retired, she had scored more international goals than any other player, male or female, with 158 goals!

Mia also co-founded the Women's United Soccer Association (WUSA) in 2000, the first professional women's soccer league in the U.S. She played for Washington Freedom in the WUSA until it folded in 2003. Even after retiring, Mia kept inspiring people. She started the Mia Hamm Foundation to support young athletes and raise awareness for bone marrow diseases, in honor of her brother Garrett. She is such a hero to so many young girls (and boys!) who love soccer and sports.

Mia Hamm showed everyone that girls can be amazing athletes and that with hard work and passion, you can achieve great things! She made soccer super popular in the U.S. and inspired a whole generation of players. Yay, Mia Hamm!

The Mia Hamm Effect

Once upon a time, girls weren't always allowed to play sports like soccer. Can you imagine that? No fun games with friends on the field, no exciting goals, and no cheering from the sidelines. Girls just didn't have the same chances as boys. How would you feel? I would feel super sad and bored.

The good news is, Mia Hamm changed that for girls!

That's right! Along came Mia Hamm, who loved soccer more than anything. She started playing when she was just a little girl, and she played so well that everyone noticed her.

Mia Hamm did so much to encourage girls to play soccer! First, she showed everyone that girls could be just as amazing at soccer. She scored tons of goals and won big championships, like the World Cup and Olympic gold medals. Imagine how cool it must have been to watch her play!

Speaking of championships, Mia helped the U.S. Women's National Team win the World Cup not once, but twice! And they also snagged Olympic gold medals in 1996 and 2004. Those wins were history-making moments that showed girls everywhere that they could achieve their dreams in sports.

And get this: Mia's fame made women's soccer more popular than ever! She was a shining star, bringing lots of attention to the sport. More girls wanted to join in and play because they saw Mia doing her thing on the field.

But wait, there's more! In 2000, Mia helped start the Women's United Soccer Association (WUSA). It was the very first professional women's soccer league in the U.S. Can you imagine how exciting it must have been for girls to see their heroes playing professionally?

Mia didn't stop there. Nope! She also started the Mia Hamm Foundation. This awesome foundation helps girls in sports and raises awareness about bone marrow diseases. So not only was she a soccer superstar, but she was also a real-life hero off the field too! And Mia always had the best advice. She encouraged kids to play soccer because they loved it, not because anyone else wanted them to. She believed in following your passions and never giving up on your dreams. What a great role model!

Plus, Mia wasn't just famous for playing soccer. She also spent time with young players at clinics, camps, and events. Can you imagine getting tips and encouragement from someone as awesome as Mia Hamm? It would be like a dream come true!

So, thanks to Mia Hamm, girls everywhere got to kick, score, and dream big on the soccer field. She showed us that with hard work, determination, and a lot of love for the game, anything is possible! Mia Hamm truly is a soccer legend and a hero to girls everywhere.

A Champion for Equality

You see, when Mia was playing, girls didn't always get the same chances as boys to play sports. But Mia thought that wasn't fair at all! So, she spoke up and fought for equal opportunities for girls in sports. She wanted everyone to have a chance to play and have fun, no matter if they were a boy or a girl.

One time, Mia noticed that girls' soccer teams didn't always get the same resources as boys' teams. So, she spoke out about it and asked for equal funding and support for girls' soccer. Because of her, more girls got the equipment, fields, and coaching they needed to play their best.

Another time, Mia noticed that girls' soccer games didn't always get as much attention as boys' games. So, she spoke up and asked for more coverage of women's sports in the media. Her words helped shine a spotlight on girls' soccer, so more people could see just how talented and exciting female athletes are.

And you know what? Mia's advocacy didn't stop there! She also pushed for equal pay for female athletes. She believed that women who worked just as hard and achieved just as much as men should be paid the same. Her efforts helped bring attention to the issue of pay inequality in sports and paved the way for positive changes in the future.

Mia's voice made a huge impact, and her fight for fairness opened doors for countless girls to play sports. Thanks to her advocacy, more girls got the chance to kick, run, and score goals, just like the boys. It's super cool because now, girls everywhere can pursue their dreams on the field, knowing that they have champions like Mia Hamm fighting for their rights and opportunities. She truly paved the way for future generations of female athletes to shine and inspire others!

A Legacy of Leadership

Mia and her teammates showed the world what it means to be a team. They were like a big group of sisters, always supporting each other through good times and tough times. Even though Mia was a superstar, she always put her team first. She didn't want all the attention just for herself; she wanted everyone to shine together.

See, Mia was always there to lift her teammates up. Whether they were facing a challenging opponent or dealing with personal struggles, Mia provided unwavering support and encouragement, showing them that they could overcome any obstacle together.

On the field, Mia led by example, demonstrating her dedication and hard work in every game and practice session. Her relentless pursuit of excellence inspired her teammates to push themselves to new heights, fostering a culture of determination and resilience within the team. As a leader, Mia was also an excellent listener. She made sure to create a safe and supportive environment where everyone's voice was heard and valued. Whether it was discussing game strategies or addressing team concerns, Mia ensured that everyone felt included and respected.

Off the field, Mia acted as a mentor and big sister to her teammates, offering guidance and support whenever they needed it. Whether it was providing advice on soccer techniques or offering a listening ear for personal issues, Mia was always there to lend a helping hand. Furthermore, Mia celebrated her teammates' successes with genuine joy and enthusiasm, recognizing that their victories were team victories. She made sure to acknowledge and appreciate everyone's contributions, fostering a sense of camaraderie and unity within the team.

In essence, Mia Hamm wasn't just a superstar athlete; she was also an incredible leader and friend. Her unwavering support, dedication, and camaraderie played a significant role in shaping the close-knit bond shared by her and her teammates, showing the world what it truly means to be part of a team.

Mia Hamm Reflection Questions

1. What do you think made Mia Hamm such a cool soccer player?

2. If you could play soccer with Mia Hamm and her friends, what would you want to learn from them?

3. If you were playing soccer with Mia Hamm, what do you think she would say to encourage you?

CHAPTER 9

MOHAMED SALAH

"Even if I see myself playing very well in one thing, I try to improve to do it better and better."

-*Mohamed Salah*

Who is Mohamed Salah?

Let me tell you all about Mohamed Salah! He's this super awesome soccer player from Egypt, and boy, can he score goals! Mohamed was born on June 15, 1992, in a place called Basyoun, which is in Egypt, not too far from Cairo.

When Salah was a little kid, he absolutely loved playing soccer. He looked up to famous players like Ronaldo and Zinedine Zidane, and he practiced their moves all the time when he played with his friends. Imagine kicking a ball around and pretending to be your favorite soccer star – that's what Salah did!

When Salah was just 14 years old, he joined a youth team called El Mokawloon. He was so good that he quickly moved up to the senior team in 2010, at just 18 years old. His amazing speed and talent caught the eye of a team in Switzerland called FC Basel, and they signed him in 2012.

After playing in Switzerland, Salah went on to play in Italy for teams like Fiorentina and AS Roma. He was a superstar there, winning awards and scoring lots of goals. Then, in 2017, he made a big move to the Premier League in England to play for Liverpool FC. That's like going from playing with your friends to playing in the biggest soccer league in the world – how cool is that?

And let me tell you, Salah didn't just play in the Premier League, he absolutely dominated! In the 2017-2018 season, he scored a whopping 32 goals, breaking the record for the most goals scored in a single season. He even helped lead Liverpool to the UEFA Champions League final – that's like the Superbowl of soccer!

Oh, and get this, Salah didn't just do amazing things on the soccer field, he also represented his country, Egypt, in big tournaments like the African Cup of Nations and the FIFA World Cup. He's a superhero for Egyptian soccer fans!

So, there you have it, Mohamed Salah is not just a soccer player, he's a legend! And his journey from a small town in Egypt to becoming one of the best players in the world is super inspiring. Who knows, maybe one day we'll see another kid from Basyoun following in his footsteps and scoring goals on the biggest stage!

The Egyptian King

Imagine this: it was a super big game, and Liverpool, the team Salah played for, was battling against their biggest rivals.

"Whoa, did you see that?!" exclaimed one of Salah's teammates, eyes wide with excitement as he watched him go!

The ball landed right at Salah's feet, and quick as a flash, he zoomed past the defenders as if they were just statues!

"I know, right? He's like lightning on the field!" another teammate replied, still in awe of Salah's incredible speed and skill.

He dribbled the ball faster than a cheetah, and then, BOOM!

"He's going for it!" shouted a third teammate, unable to contain his excitement.

He kicked it right into the goal! The whole stadium erupted with cheers and shouts, everyone screaming Salah's name because they knew they had just seen something totally awesome!

And then, as Salah scored the goal, the entire team erupted into cheers and applause.

"Yes! That's our guy!" they shouted, jumping up and down in celebration. Salah's teammates rushed over to him, patting him on the back and congratulating him.

"You're a legend, Salah!" one of them exclaimed, admiration evident in his voice. Salah just grinned, soaking in the moment.

"Thanks, guys! Couldn't have done it without you!" he replied, grateful for the support of his teammates.

As you can see, fans adore Mohamed Salah for his electrifying pace, which allows him to leave defenders trailing behind him as he dashes towards the goal. His incredible finishing ability ensures that when he gets within striking distance, there's a high chance he'll find the back of the net with precision and power.

Fans also love Mohamed Salah for his flamboyant celebrations. After scoring a goal, Salah's celebrations are a sight to behold, filled with joy and passion, often showcasing his unique style and personality, which further endears him to supporters around the world.

Let's take a closer look at these celebrations because they're so cool! When he scores, he does all these amazing things that make everyone cheer even louder! Like, one time, he did this yoga pose where he stood on one leg and put his hands together like he was praying. It looked like he was balancing perfectly, just like in yoga class! And then, in another game, he made this funny face and crossed his fingers over his nose, like he was saying, "Shhh, I scored!" It was so silly, but everyone loved it! And there's this other celebration where he stretches his arms out wide, just like he's saying, "Ta-da! Look what I did!" It's like he's showing off his superpowers! Oh, and after every goal, he always takes a moment to kneel down and pray. It's really special because it shows how thankful he is for his talent. Salah's celebrations are like his own special language on the field, and they make watching soccer even more fun!

His celebrations make the fans so happy that they call him the "Egyptian King" and make up a song to go with it! Have you heard the song? It's so catchy! They sing, "Mo Salah! Mo Salah! Mo Salah! Running down the wing. Mo Salah la-la-la la-ahh, The Egyptian King!"

Isn't that awesome? And there's another song too. It goes, "If he's good enough for you, he's good enough for me. If he scores another few, then I'll be Muslim too." Wow, that's really cool, showing support for Salah and his faith. It must feel amazing for him to hear all those fans singing his name!

Unstoppable Rise

Life wasn't always easy for Mohamed Salah. In fact, he faced quite a few challenges and setbacks during his journey to the top. One big challenge was when he first moved to England to play for Chelsea FC in 2014. Even though he was really talented, he didn't get as much playing time as he wanted, and some people doubted if he could make it in the Premier League. But Salah didn't let that get him down. Instead, he used it as motivation to work even harder. He kept training, kept pushing himself, and never gave up on his dream of becoming a top soccer player.

Another setback came when he left Chelsea and went to play for Italian teams like Fiorentina and AS Roma on loan. It wasn't easy adapting to a new country and a new style of play, but Salah didn't let that stop him either. He kept proving himself on the field, scoring goals and showing everyone what he was capable of.

And finally, there were times when Salah faced criticism and doubt, especially during his early days at Liverpool. But he didn't let the haters get to him. Instead, he let his performance do the talking, and soon enough, he silenced all the doubters with his incredible skills and goal-scoring ability.

So yeah, Mohamed Salah faced plenty of challenges and setbacks along the way, but he never let them stop him from reaching his goals. He kept believing in himself and working hard, and eventually, he became one of the best soccer players in the world! Mohamed Salah's rise in soccer was like a superhero story! Starting from the bottom, facing tough challenges and setbacks, but never giving up. He just kept going, getting better and better with each game. He rose to the top and did not let anything get in his way.

A Role Model for Aspiring Athletes

Mohamed Salah's work ethic, humility, and dedication to his craft are legendary tales in the world of soccer! I mean, this guy puts in the extra hours on the training ground, always striving to improve his skills and make a difference on the field.

Even when he faces criticism or setbacks, he doesn't let it get him down. Instead, he uses it as fuel to push himself even harder. And you know what? It pays off big time! But what's really amazing is how humble Salah stays, despite all his success. He doesn't let fame or fortune go to his head. He's always grateful for his opportunities and never forgets where he came from.

For instance, even though he's scored countless goals and won numerous awards, he always credits his teammates and coaches for their support. He never seeks the spotlight for himself but instead shares the glory with those around him.

Additionally, Salah is known for his charitable work off the field. He regularly donates to various causes and uses his platform to raise awareness for important issues. Some charities that he works with are the Nile Hospital in Egypt, supporting healthcare. Salah has also supported Tawasol Charity, an organization that focuses on schools for children in Egypt. Along with that, Salah has participated in various initiatives organized by the Liverpool

FC Foundation, which works to create positive change in the lives of children and young people through sports and education. Not to mention his involvement with the Egyptian Football Federation, supporting projects that aim to help soccer talent and promote the sport in Egypt. All of this shows that he's not just focused on his own success but also on making a positive impact in the world.

Moreover, Salah is always gracious in victory and humble in defeat. Whether his team wins or loses, he handles himself with dignity and respect, never boasting or complaining. This attitude endears him to fans and earns him the respect of his peers, demonstrating that true greatness is measured not only by talent but also by character.

Mohamed Salah Reflection Questions

1. If you could meet Mohamed Salah, what would you ask him?

2. Why do you think Mohamed Salah helps charities and gives back to his community?

┌───┐
│   │
│   │
│   │
│   │
│   │
└───┘

3. What lesson do you think we can learn from Mohamed Salah's life and career?

┌───┐
│   │
│   │
│   │
│   │
└───┘

CHAPTER 10

KEVIN DE BRUYNE

"I think the goal is to win everything. Whatever we can reach is nice to take."

-Kevin De Bruyne

Who is Kevin De Bruyne?

Let me tell you about Kevin De Bruyne! He's like a soccer superstar, but way cooler! Picture this: it's June 28, 1991, and boom, Kevin is born in Drongen, Belgium. That's where his journey to greatness starts! Fast forward to 2012, Kevin joins Chelsea FC. Woohoo!

But wait, there's more! In January 2014, he moved to Wolfsburg, Germany, and joined the Bundesliga. He's unstoppable!

But hold on to your hats because in August 2015, Manchester City snatched him up. And guess what? He became a midfield maestro, scoring goals and making amazing assists!

And in 2020, he was crowned the Premier League Player of the Season. Can you believe it? That's like the ultimate trophy for being awesome at soccer!

He also won the UEFA Champions League in 2023, and was one of the most critical players on the team!

But wait, there's a cherry on top! Kevin lead Belgium to the semi-finals in the 2018 FIFA World Cup. Whoa! Talk about representing your country like a boss!

Oh, and did I mention there's a killer move called the "De Bruyne assist"? It's like magic on the field! So, there you have it, folks! Kevin De Bruyne, the soccer sensation, living his dream and making us all go wild with his epic skills and achievements!

The Architect of Attacks

Kevin loved playing soccer more than anything else in the world. Every day after school, he would rush to the park with his friends to kick the ball around.

One sunny afternoon, while playing with his friends, Kevin noticed something special about the way he played. He wasn't just kicking the ball randomly; he was thinking about where to pass it next and how to create opportunities to score goals. His friends noticed it too!

"Hey, Kevin, how do you always know where to pass the ball?" asked his friend Jake.

Kevin shrugged and replied, "I don't know. I just see it in my head, like a picture of the game unfolding."

From that day on, Kevin's friends started calling him "The Architect" because he was like a master builder, constructing attacks and creating chances for his team.

As Kevin grew older, his love for soccer only deepened. He practiced tirelessly, working on his passing, shooting, and vision on the pitch. He dreamed of one day playing for his favorite team, Manchester City, and becoming a famous soccer player.

Kevin's dream came true when he was spotted by a talent scout from Manchester City while playing for his local club. He was invited to join their youth academy, where he continued to impress everyone with his skills and tactical intelligence.

Years passed, and Kevin eventually made it to the first team of Manchester City. He became known for his talent and as the mastermind behind their attacks. With his precise passes and clever movement on the pitch, he orchestrated goal after goal, leading his team to victory after victory.

One day, after scoring a breathtaking goal in a crucial match, Kevin's coach approached him with a smile.

"Kevin, you truly are the architect of our attacks. Your vision and creativity make you a special player, and I'm proud to have you on our team."

With a grin, Kevin replied, "Thanks, coach. I just love playing soccer and helping my team win. Being called 'The Architect' is just the icing on the cake."

And from that day on, Kevin De Bruyne continued to dazzle soccer fans around the world with his brilliant play, forever remembered as the little boy who became the architect of attacks.

And the park where it all began? Well, it's now known as "Kevin's Playground," where young soccer players come to hone their skills and dream of following in his footsteps.

From Doubt to Domination

But Kevin's journey wasn't easy. When he was just a young lad, he embarked on a thrilling adventure with Chelsea FC, one of the biggest clubs in England. Oh, the excitement he felt, pulling on that famous blue jersey for the first time! But alas, his joy was short-lived.

The coach, a stern figure on the sidelines, didn't always choose him to play. Kevin would sit on the bench, his heart sinking with each passing minute. He longed to feel the grass beneath his boots, to hear the roar of the crowd as he chased the ball. But instead, he watched from the sidelines, his dreams just out of reach.

Then, one day, Chelsea decided to loan Kevin to a team in Germany. Werder Bremen welcomed him with open arms, and Kevin knew this was his chance to shine. With determination burning bright in his eyes, he poured his heart and soul into every training session, every match.

And oh, how he dazzled! With each flick of his boot, each burst of speed, Kevin wowed the crowds and left defenders in his wake. Goals flowed from his feet, and his teammates marveled at his skill. Suddenly, everyone was talking about him, the boy wonder from Belgium who had conquered Germany's Bundesliga.

But when Kevin returned to Chelsea, hoping for a hero's welcome, he was met with disappointment. Once again, he found himself relegated to the bench, watching as others took to the field in his place. It was a bitter pill to swallow, and Kevin felt his dreams slipping away.

But he refused to give up. Determined to carve out a path of his own, Kevin made the bold decision to leave Chelsea behind.

He packed his bags and headed to VfL Wolfsburg, where a new chapter awaited. And oh, what a chapter it would be!

In the green and white of Wolfsburg, Kevin found his stride. With each match, he silenced the doubters and proved his worth. Goals flowed freely from his boots, and his name echoed through stadiums across Europe. He was no longer just a promising talent; he was a force to be reckoned with.

And then, like a beacon in the night, Manchester City came calling. It was a dream come true for Kevin, a chance to play for one of the best teams in the world. With renewed determination, he set about making his mark on English football.

With his mesmerizing passes and clever tricks, Kevin became the heartbeat of Manchester City's midfield. Trophies followed in his wake, and his name was etched into the annals of soccer history. But amidst the glory, Kevin never forgot the journey that had brought him here — the challenges faced, the obstacles overcome.

Kevin De Bruyne was more than just a soccer player. He was a symbol of resilience, a testament to the power of perseverance. And as his star continued to rise, he inspired countless others to chase their dreams, no matter the obstacles in their path.

The Power of Perseverance

Kevin De Bruyne's journey from facing challenges to becoming a soccer superstar is a thrilling adventure story! It's all about never giving up and chasing your dreams with all your might.

Kevin's story shows us that setbacks are just bumps in the road, not dead ends. Even when things didn't go his way, like not playing much at Chelsea, he didn't let it stop him. Instead, he used it as motivation to push himself even harder. That's the spirit!

Next, Kevin's bravery to try new things teaches us that sometimes you have to take a leap of faith. Leaving Chelsea for VfL Wolfsburg was a big step into the unknown, but it turned out to be his big break! It reminds us that stepping out of our comfort zones can lead to amazing adventures.

And let's not forget about Kevin's dedication to getting better every single day. He didn't become a superstar overnight. It took loads of practice, sweat, and determination to reach the top. His story tells us that with hard work and perseverance, we can achieve anything we set our minds to.

In the end, Kevin De Bruyne's journey teaches us that no matter how tough things get, never lose sight of your dreams. Keep pushing forward, stay determined, and believe in yourself. Who knows? You might just score the winning goal of your own adventure!

Kevin De Bruyne Reflection Questions

1. What challenges did Kevin De Bruyne face in his soccer journey, and how did he overcome them?

2. What do you think Kevin De Bruyne's story teaches us about the power of believing in ourselves?

3. Have you ever had to try something new and scary, like Kevin did when he left Chelsea for VfL Wolfsburg? How did it turn out?

CHAPTER 11

MARTA

"We all have obstacles. The feeling of satisfaction comes by overcoming something."

-Marta

Who is Marta?

Let me tell you all about the amazing Marta! She is a soccer superstar from Brazil, and her full name is Marta Vieira da Silva. She was born on February 19, 1986, in a small town called Dois Riachos in Alagoas, Brazil. From a young age, Marta loved playing soccer, even though not many girls played the sport back then. She played in a place called Jacaré dos Homens, which means "Alligator of Men," because it was mostly boys who played there.

Marta's journey in soccer started with a club called Vasco da Gama. She was so talented that she soon moved to Sweden to play for Umeå IK, where she became a superstar. She later played for Tyresö FF and Rosengård, also in Sweden. Marta didn't stop there—she played for several teams in the United States too, including Los Angeles Sol, Western New York Flash, Gold Pride, and finally Orlando Pride, where she's been since 2017.

Now, let's talk about her international career with Brazil. Marta is the highest-scoring player in Brazilian history for both men and women, with an incredible 116 goals in 175 matches! She has also scored more goals in the FIFA Women's World Cup than anyone else—17 goals in six tournaments!

Marta has won many awards, too. She was named the best player in the world six times: in 2006, 2007, 2008, 2009, 2010, and 2018. Isn't that amazing? She even received the FIFA Special Award in January 2024 for her outstanding career achievements.

Marta's skill and dedication have earned her the nickname "Queen Marta." She helped Brazil win three Copa America

Femenina titles and silver medals in the 2004 and 2008 Olympics. Marta is also a hero and an inspiration for many young girls around the world who dream of playing soccer. She showed that with hard work and determination, you can achieve your dreams no matter where you come from. In 2025, FIFA will introduce the "Marta Award," given to the player who scores the best goal in women's soccer, to honor her legacy.

Marta's story is about more than just soccer; it's about breaking barriers, inspiring others, and being a true champion on and off the field.

The Queen of Football

Marta never imagined she'd one day be known as the "Queen of Soccer." As a young girl, she played soccer in the streets of Jacaré dos Homens with a passion that would later lead her to be a symbol of female soccer worldwide.

She got that wonderful title on a historic day in 2007. Marta, with her boots laced tight and her heart brimming with determination, graced the field in the FIFA Women's World Cup. She helped her team win 3-2. After the game, her teammate said, "Marta, you're so smart on the field. You're like a queen!"

Next, Brazil faced the United States in the semifinals. It was a tough game, but Marta encouraged her teammates at halftime, saying, "We've come so far, let's keep going!" Brazil scored four goals in the second half and won 4-0.

Then came the final match against Germany. Brazil played really well and won 2-0. After the game, the team captain told Marta, "You're our leader. This win is for you, Queen Marta!"

After Brazil won, everyone in the country celebrated. People chanted Marta's name, and she became a hero to young girls who wanted to play soccer. Her journey showed them that anything is possible if you work hard.

Now, she is revered not just in Brazil but around the globe.

"Marta, your vision is incredible!" everyone exclaimed.

No matter what, Marta continued to shine. Her precise passes and quick thinking led to win after win.

Her teammates often remarked, "With Marta leading us, we feel unstoppable."

As Marta looked back on all her World Cup plays, she felt a great sense of accomplishment. She had not only proven herself as a player but had also helped bring women's soccer to new heights. Her teammates' words echoed in her mind, a testament to her impact on and off the pitch: "Marta, our Queen of Soccer."

Breaking Barriers

While Marta loved playing soccer with the boys in the dusty streets, it wasn't easy. One boy said, "Girls shouldn't play soccer." Marta, with fire in her eyes, replied, "I'll show you girls can play just as well as boys!"

As she got older, Marta moved to Rio de Janeiro to chase her dream of becoming a professional soccer player. Things were tough there too. Coaches ignored her, and she didn't get the same support as the boys. But Marta didn't give up. She practiced every day, even after everyone else went home. One day, a coach finally noticed her. "You have something special, Marta," he said. "But you'll need to work twice as hard as the boys."

Marta worked even harder. In a big game for her local club, she scored three goals and led her team to victory. Her teammates lifted her up, cheering, "Marta! Marta!" But Marta knew her journey was just beginning.

Soon, Marta was playing for Brazil's national team. But the challenges kept coming. During an international tour, she overheard someone say, "The Brazilian team is strong, but they have a girl leading them." This made Marta even more determined. She scored two goals and helped her team win. After the match, another teammate said, "Marta, you inspire all of us. You show that we belong here."

As Marta became more famous, she spoke out about how women's soccer needed to be treated better. "We deserve the same respect as the men," she said. "The young girls watching us need to see that their dreams are important."

Marta became a hero for young girls all around the world. Once, she visited a school in Brazil, and a little girl ran up to her and said, "Marta, I want to be just like you!" Marta smiled and replied, "You can be even better. Believe in yourself and never give up, no matter what anyone says."

Her influence spread far beyond Brazil. During a training camp in the United States, a young player approached her and said, "Marta, your story gives me hope. You've shown me that it's possible to succeed despite the challenges." Marta smiled and replied, "Always remember that your passion and hard work will speak louder than any obstacles you face."

Throughout her career, Marta broke records and won many awards. As we know, she was called the "Queen of Soccer," a title she wore proudly. But for Marta, the best part was inspiring the next generation. "If my journey can make it easier for even one girl to follow her dreams," she said, "then everything I've faced has been worth it."

When Marta decided to retire from international soccer, she had left a huge mark on the sport. Her legacy was not just in her goals and victories, but in the countless girls around the world who looked up to her and saw their own potential. As she walked off the field for the last time, she saw hundreds of young faces cheering her on. In that moment, Marta knew she had truly made a difference.

A Champion for the Beautiful Game

Marta is a superhero for women's soccer! She uses her massive online following and goes to events all around the world to help young players and make soccer better for everyone.

On Instagram and Twitter, Marta talks to millions of fans. She shares videos and tips about playing soccer. Marta cheers on female athletes and talks about why it's important for girls to have the same chances in sports. In her videos, she tells girls to believe in themselves and never give up. For instance, she might share a video of herself performing a cool soccer trick and then say, "You can do it too! Keep practicing!"

Marta also goes to schools and soccer programs to meet kids who love the game. She tells them about her own challenges and how she kept going. Marta says hard work and loving what you do are key. She tells kids that even when things are tough, they can get stronger and better. Once, she visited a school in Brazil where she grew up, and she talked to the kids about how she used to play soccer in the streets with her friends when she was their age.

She works with groups that support women's sports, like the United Nations. Marta tells leaders that girls need more help in soccer. She wants better fields, more games on TV, and more girls' teams. Marta says it's not fair that girls don't get the same chances as boys. She wants every girl to have the chance to play and be a star on the soccer field. Last year, she joined a campaign with the UN to help girls in Brazil learn soccer skills and get the chance to play in real games.

Marta's not just a great player... she's also a champion for women's soccer, on and off the field!

Marta Reflection Questions

1. What do you admire most about Marta's soccer career and why?

2. How do you think Marta's determination and passion for the game have inspired other young players?

3. In what ways do you think Marta has helped make soccer more inclusive for girls around the world?

CHAPTER 12

CHRISTINE SINCLAIR

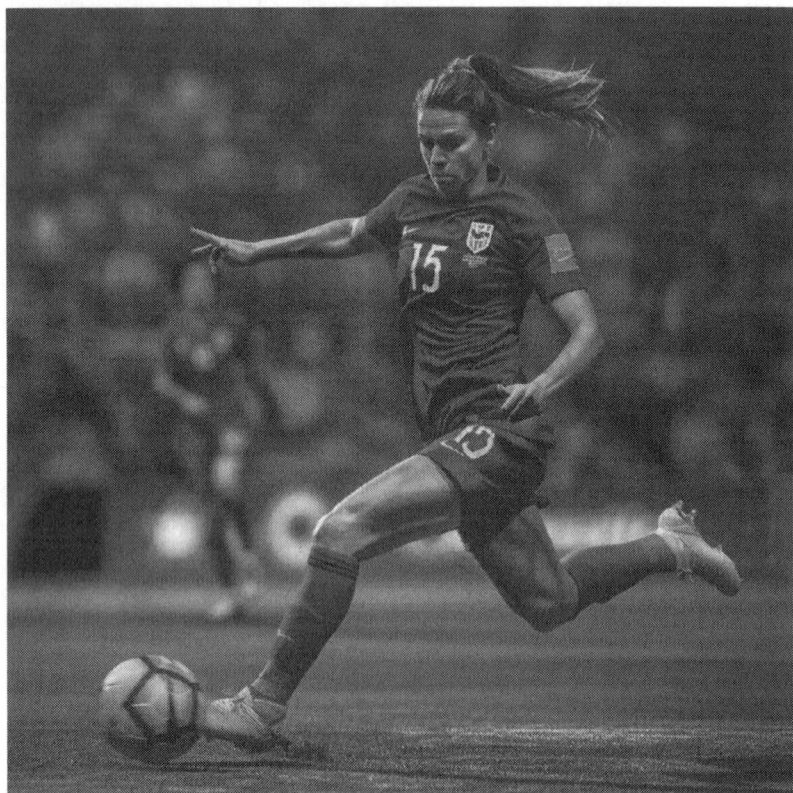

"I think the thing that has sort of always separated me,

even from when I was younger, is my ability to score goals."

-Christine Sinclair

Who is Christine Sinclair?

Let me tell you all about Christine Sinclair! She's an amazing soccer superstar from Canada, and her story is super cool!

So, Christine Sinclair was born on June 12, 1983, in Burnaby, British Columbia, which is in Canada, of course. She's been playing soccer since she was four years old! Can you even imagine that? She started out in her hometown, just kicking the ball around with her friends, a total natural.

In high school, she led her team to three league championship wins! That's winning the biggest trophy three times in a row! Then, she went to the University of Portland and studied biology while playing soccer. She graduated in 2005, which means she's not just super talented on the field, she's smart too!

Now, let's talk about her soccer career because it's seriously impressive. Christine has been playing for the Women's Canadian Soccer Team for ages, and she's their all-time leading goal scorer! She's been part of four World Cups (in 2003, 2007, 2011, and 2015) and two Olympics (in 2008 and 2012). Oh, and she's won all sorts of awards too, like the Hermann Trophy in 2004 and 2005, which is a big deal in college soccer.

But wait, there's more! Christine is tough as nails. Like, seriously. During the Women's World Cup in 2011, she broke her nose in the first game! Can you believe that? But did she give up? Nope! She kept playing with a face mask to protect her nose. That's dedication right there!

And get this, she's also a national hero! In 2012, she won a bronze medal at the Olympics in Rio, representing Canada. Plus, she's been named Canadian Soccer Association Player of the Year a whopping 11 times! That's like, winning the coolest award over and over again!

So yeah, Christine Sinclair is basically the coolest soccer player ever. She's talented, tough, and a total inspiration to kids all around the world!

The All-Time Leading Scorer

Christine Sinclair stood on the field, her heart racing with excitement. She knew she was on the verge of making history. As the game kicked off, she could feel the anticipation building among the crowd.

On the sideline, her coach watched with a proud smile.

"This is it, Christine," he said, clapping her on the back. "You've worked so hard for this moment. Now go out there and make it count."

Christine nodded, her determination shining in her eyes. She had been dreaming of this moment since she was a little girl kicking a soccer ball around in her backyard. Now, with the support of her teammates and fans, she was ready to make her mark on the world.

As the game progressed, Christine played with fierce intensity. She fought for every ball, determined to seize her moment of glory. And then, halfway through the second half, it happened.

The ball came soaring towards Christine, and without hesitation, she launched herself into the air. With a powerful header, she sent the ball rocketing towards the net. Time seemed to stand still as the ball sailed past the goalkeeper and into the back of the net.

The stadium erupted into cheers as Christine's teammates rushed to congratulate her. Tears welled up in her eyes as she realized what she had just achieved. She had scored her 190th international goal, breaking the record for the most goals scored by any soccer player.

After the game, Christine was surrounded by reporters eager to capture her thoughts on her historic achievement.

"I'm just so grateful to have had the opportunity to represent my country on the world stage," she said, her voice trembling with emotion. "This record is a testament to the hard work and dedication of everyone who has supported me along the way."

As she stood on the field, basking in the glow of her victory, Christine knew that this moment would stay with her forever. She had achieved her lifelong dream of becoming the greatest soccer player in the world, and nothing could ever take that away from her.

Leading by Example

Christine wasn't just any soccer player, oh no! She was a leader, on and off the field. She would zip across the field with lightning speed, kicking the ball with precision and skill. But what made her really special was her heart. She had the biggest heart on the team, and she always put her teammates first.

One day, during practice, Christine's coach asked her to lead a special drill.

"I need you to show the team how to dribble the ball like a pro," he said, looking at her with a twinkle in his eye.

Christine nodded eagerly and gathered her teammates around her. "Okay, everyone," she said with a big smile. "Watch closely, and I'll show you how it's done!"

She dribbled the ball around the cones with grace and ease, her teammates cheering her on. And then, one by one, they took turns trying to imitate her moves. Christine encouraged them every step of the way, offering tips and advice to help them improve.

After practice, Christine stayed behind to help clean up the field.

"Teamwork makes the dream work, right?" she said, flashing her teammates a thumbs up.

But Christine wasn't just a leader on the field. She was also a leader in her community. She spent her free time volunteering at local schools, teaching kids about the importance of teamwork and perseverance.

One day, she visited a school where the soccer team was feeling down after losing a big game. Christine listened to their stories and shared her own experiences of overcoming challenges on the field.

"It's okay to lose sometimes," she told them gently. "What matters is that you never give up and keep working hard to achieve your goals."

The kids looked up at Christine with wide eyes, inspired by her words. They vowed to keep practicing and never lose hope, just like their superhero soccer player.

And so, Christine Sinclair continued to lead by example, both on and off the field. With her work ethic, commitment to her team, and unwavering determination, she inspired everyone around her to believe in themselves and reach for greatness. And that, my friends, is what makes her a true leader.

A Global Ambassador

However, Christine Sinclair is not limited to scoring goals and winning games. Nope! She's all about teamwork, sportsmanship, and believing in yourself. She's a real-life superhero, but instead of wearing a cape, she wears soccer cleats!

One time, Christine visited a school to talk to kids about soccer and being a good teammate. She told them how important it was to support each other, even when things got tough. And you know what? The kids loved it! They were so inspired by her words that they started their own soccer team and named it after her. How cool is that?

But wait, there's more! Christine also does a lot of charity work. She spends her free time helping out in her community and raising money for important causes. Like, one time, she organized a charity soccer game to raise money for kids who couldn't afford to play sports. And you know what? They raised tons of money and helped so many kids get a chance to play the game they love.

Oh, and have you seen the custom Barbie doll of Christine Sinclair? It's seriously awesome! It looks just like her, with her soccer jersey and everything. It's a personal mini Christine Sinclair to play with!

So yeah, Christine Sinclair is not just a soccer player. She's a role model who shows kids everywhere that with hard work, determination, and a little bit of teamwork, you can achieve anything you set your mind to. She's proof that girls can be super awesome at sports, and that's pretty amazing if you ask me!

Christine Sinclair Reflection Questions

1. What do you think makes Christine Sinclair such a great role model for kids?

2. How do you think Christine's message about teamwork and sportsmanship can help you in your own life, on and off the soccer field?

3. If you could ask Christine Sinclair one question about her soccer career or charity work, what would it be?

CHAPTER 13

FRENKIE DE JONG

"I try not to pay attention to talk of comparisons. I only want to focus on myself."

-Frenkie de Jong

Who is Frenkie de Jong?

Once, in a little village called Arkel, there was a boy named Frenkie de Jong. He loved kicking around a soccer ball since he was just a little boy. When he was six, his dad took him to join the ASV Arkel soccer club. Imagine tiny Frenkie running around with his friends, chasing that ball with all his might!

Then, when he was eight, something amazing happened! Frenkie got scouted by a big soccer club called Willem II. It was like a dream come true! He packed up his soccer cleats and headed to Tilburg to join their youth academy. That was in 2005, can you believe it? He was just a little guy!

Fast forward to 2013, and Frenkie was ready to take his soccer journey to the next level. At just sixteen years old, he signed his very first professional contract with Willem II. Can you imagine being a pro athlete at sixteen? That's super impressive!

But wait, there's more! On May 10th, 2015, Frenkie made his big debut as a professional soccer player for Willem II, just two days before his eighteenth birthday. He must have been so excited to step onto that field and show everyone what he could do!

Then, in 2016, Frenkie got the chance of a lifetime. He joined Ajax, another big soccer club. It was a dream come true for him! And get this, he made his debut for Ajax on September 21st, 2016. That's a day he'll never forget!

But Frenkie didn't stop there. Oh no, he kept working hard and showing everyone what he was made of. In 2018, he really started to shine. He became a regular starter for Ajax and stood out as an amazing midfielder. Plus, he even made his debut for the Dutch National Team that year. Talk about reaching for the stars!

Then, in 2019, Frenkie's dreams came true again. He signed with FC Barcelona, one of the biggest soccer clubs in the world! Can you imagine playing for Barcelona? It's absolutely amazing!

And guess what? Frenkie didn't just play for Barcelona, he won prizes too! In his first year with the team, he helped them win the cup and the national title. He even made it to the semi-finals of the Champions League! That's like the Superbowl of soccer!

So, there you have it, the amazing story of Frenkie de Jong. From kicking a ball around in his hometown to playing for some of the biggest clubs in the world, he's shown that with hard work and determination, you can achieve anything you set your mind to!

The Composed Maestro

In the buzzing stadium, little Timmy watched with wide eyes as his hero, Frenkie de Jong, took to the field. Excitement bubbled in his chest as he cheered for his favorite player, hoping to see some magical moments unfold.

But as the game progressed, Timmy's excitement turned to worry. Frenkie seemed off his game, missing passes and struggling to find his rhythm. "Oh no," Timmy muttered, his heart sinking as he watched his hero falter.

On the pitch, Frenkie could feel the pressure mounting. Passes that usually flowed effortlessly from his feet were now going astray, and the frustration was building. But amidst the chaos, Frenkie remained composed.

"Come on, Frenkie!" Timmy shouted from the stands, trying to encourage his hero. But Frenkie seemed unfazed by the cheers and jeers echoing around him. Instead, he focused on the game, determined to turn things around.

As the match continued, Frenkie's composure became more evident. Despite the setbacks, he refused to let it bother him. He shrugged off each missed pass and focused on the next opportunity.

"You can do it, Frenkie!" Timmy yelled, his voice filled with hope. And just when it seemed like all was lost, Frenkie's moment came. With a sudden burst of energy, he surged forward, weaving through defenders with ease.

The crowd erupted into cheers as Frenkie unleashed a perfect through ball, setting up his teammate for a goal. Timmy jumped up and down in excitement, his worries forgotten as he watched his hero shine once again.

Frenkie may have had a rough start, but his unwavering composure and determination won the day. As the final whistle blew, Timmy couldn't help but feel proud of his hero. "Frenkie is the best!" he exclaimed, his voice filled with admiration. And in that moment, he knew that no matter what challenges came his way, Frenkie would always rise above them.

The Barcelona Legacy

Frenkie's journey to Barcelona is like something out of a movie! He was just this kid in the Netherlands, you know? Playing soccer with his friends and dreaming big. And then, bam! He started getting really good at soccer, like seriously good!

And guess what happened next? Barcelona, yes, Barcelona, the super-duper famous club, noticed him! Can you believe it? They were like, "Hey Frenkie, you're amazing! Wanna come play for us?" And Frenkie was like, "Uh, yeah, totally!"

So, off he went to Barcelona, leaving his home in the Netherlands behind. And let me tell you, he fit right in! It's like he was born to play for Barcelona!

Now Frenkie's out there on the field, wearing the iconic Barcelona jersey and showing everyone what he's made of. He's dribbling past defenders, making amazing passes, and being a soccer sensation!

I mean, can you imagine? From a kid playing soccer in the Netherlands to a superstar at FC Barcelona! It's a dream come true! And Frenkie's living that dream every single day! Isn't that just the coolest thing ever? Go Frenkie!

The Future is Bright

Frenkie de Jong is a super amazing soccer player with so much potential! Like, seriously, he's gonna be a big deal in the soccer world for, like, forever!

So, here's the scoop: Frenkie's not just your average player. Nah, he's got something special, something that makes all the experts go, "Wow!" His skills on the field are out of this world! He can dribble past defenders like they're not even there, and his passing? Oh boy, don't even get me started! It's like he's got eyes in the back of his head or something!

But it's not just about his skills, you know? Frenkie's got this amazing soccer brain too! He's always thinking ahead, planning his next move before anyone else even knows what's happening. It's like he's playing chess while everyone else is playing checkers!

And here's the really cool part: Frenkie's still super young! Like, he's got his whole soccer career ahead of him, and trust me, he's gonna make the most of it! With his talent and determination, there's no doubt in my mind that he's gonna be a dominant force in the soccer world for years to come!

So, mark my words: Frenkie de Jong is gonna be a name you'll be hearing a lot about in the future. Remember I told you!

Frenkie de Jong Reflection Questions

1. How do you think Frenkie de Jong felt when he went from playing soccer with his friends to joining one of the most legendary clubs in the world?

2. How do you think Frenkie felt when he got the incredible opportunity to play for an amazing team like Barcelona? Do you think he was nervous, excited, or maybe a little bit of both?

3. Frenkie's story shows us that with hard work and dedication, we can turn our dreams into reality. What dreams do you have, and what steps can you take to make them come true, just like Frenkie did with his dream of playing in the big leagues?

CHAPTER 14

ZINEDINE ZIDANE

"Life is full of regrets, but it doesn't pay to look back."

-Zinedine Zidane

Who is Zinedine Zidane?

Wow, have you ever heard of Zinedine Zidane? He's like a soccer superhero! Let me tell you all about his amazing life!

Okay, so picture this: Zidane was born on June 23, 1972, in Marseille, France. That's like a bazillion years ago, but he's still super cool! As a kid, he was dribbling soccer balls around the streets of Marseille, dreaming of becoming a soccer legend. And guess what? He totally did!

In 1989, when he was just a little older than me, Zidane started playing for this team called Cannes. He was only 17! Can you imagine being that good at soccer when you're still in high school?

Then, in 1996, Zidane joined Juventus, this super famous Italian soccer team. He was like a soccer wizard on the field, casting spells with his fancy footwork and magical passes. And get this: in 1998, he won the Ballon d'Or, which is an MVP award for soccer!

But wait, it gets even better! In 2001, Zidane's dream came true when he signed with Real Madrid. That's like the Hogwarts of soccer teams! And guess what happened next? He scored the winning goal in the 2002 Champions League final! It was like something out of a fairy tale!

And you know what's really cool? Even after he retired from playing, Zidane stayed with Real Madrid as a coach. He led them to three more Champions League titles! I mean, talk about a soccer legend!

So yeah, that's the story of Zinedine Zidane, the soccer superstar who went from kicking a ball around the streets of Marseille to winning championships with Real Madrid! He's like the coolest soccer player ever!

The French Maestro

One day, Zidane was playing in the 2002 World Cup final, and let me tell you, it was like something out of a fairy tale!

Zidane was on the field, wearing his National French Jersey with the whole world watching. And then, out of nowhere, the ball came flying towards him! He jumped up high, like a superhero taking flight, and with a swing of his foot, he sent the ball flying!

As the ball sailed through the air, Zidane's teammates held their breath, and the fans in the stadium screamed with excitement. And then, it happened! Zidane's foot met the ball perfectly, and it flew into the net with a swish!

"Goal!" shouted the commentator, and the crowd erupted into cheers. Zidane ran across the field, his arms raised high, with the biggest grin on his face. "We did it!" he shouted to his teammates, who were jumping up and down with joy.

And that, my friends, was Zinedine Zidane's iconic volley in the 2002 World Cup final. It was a moment of pure magic, and Zidane was the hero of the day! This showed that he wasn't just any soccer player – he was a true legend, known for his elegance and grace on the field. His passing vision was like no other; he could spot a teammate making a run from miles away and send them the perfect ball with just a flick of his foot.

And his technical mastery? Oh boy, let me tell you, it was out of this world! Zidane could dribble past defenders with ease, leaving them trailing in his wake like some kind of soccer wizard. And when it came to scoring goals, well, let's just say Zidane had a knack for the spectacular.

But you know what was really special about Zinedine Zidane? It wasn't just his skill on the field – it was the way he played with so much passion and joy. Every time he stepped onto the pitch, you could see the love he had for the game shining in his eyes. And that, my friends, is what made him truly iconic.

From the Streets to Stardom

Every day after school, young Zidane would rush outside with his friends to play soccer in the streets.

"Hey, Zidane, pass the ball!" shouted his friend Pierre, as they kicked the ball back and forth.

Zidane dribbled the ball with fancy footwork, weaving in and out of imaginary defenders. "Watch this!" he exclaimed, as he performed a tricky move that left his friends in awe.

"Wow, Zidane, you're amazing!" cheered his friend.

Zidane grinned and continued to show off his skills, dreaming of one day playing for a big team like Real Madrid. Little did he know, playing street soccer would be the foundation for his incredible journey to greatness.

As Zidane's reputation grew, more and more people came to watch him play in the narrow alleyways and makeshift pitches of his neighborhood. His dazzling footwork and precise passes left spectators in awe, and soon whispers of his talent spread beyond the streets of Marseille.

One day, as Zidane was practicing his moves, a scout from a local soccer club happened to be passing by. Impressed by what he saw, the scout approached Zidane with an offer.

"Hey there, young man! I couldn't help but notice your skills. Have you ever thought about playing for a real team?" the scout asked with a friendly smile.

Zidane's eyes widened in disbelief. Could this be his big break?

"Me? Play for a real team?" he stammered, hardly daring to believe his luck.

"That's right! We could use someone like you on our youth squad. What do you say?" the scout said, his excitement growing.

Zidane didn't have to think twice. With a grin as wide as the goalposts, he eagerly accepted the offer.

From that day on, Zidane's life changed forever. He traded the dusty streets for the pristine pitches of the soccer academy, where he continued to dazzle coaches and teammates with his incredible talent.

But no matter how far he went in his soccer career, Zidane never forgot his roots. He always remembered the humble beginnings that shaped him into the player he had become, grateful for the opportunities that street soccer had given him.

A Leader on and Off the Pitch

Zidane wasn't just good at kicking the ball; he was also really great at leading his team!

You see, whenever Zidane stepped onto the field, his teammates knew that they could count on him. He wasn't just about scoring goals or making fancy moves. No way! Zidane was like the glue that held his team together. He encouraged them when they were feeling down, and he celebrated with them when they scored.

But Zidane's leadership skills didn't stop there. Oh no! After he retired from playing soccer, he decided to become a coach. And guess what? He was super good at that too!

As a coach, Zidane used all the things he learned as a player to help his team succeed. He knew how to motivate them and how to make them play their best. And you know what else? He led his team to win lots of trophies, just like he did when he was playing!

So, Zinedine Zidane wasn't just a soccer player. He was a leader on and off the field. And even though he's not playing anymore, his influence on the game will never be forgotten! Go Zidane!

Zinedine Zidane Reflection Questions

1. What parts of Zinedine Zidane's childhood helped him become a great soccer player?

2. How did Zinedine Zidane's fancy moves and smart thinking help him win games?

3. What can we learn from Zinedine Zidane about never giving up, even when things get tough?

CHAPTER 15

WESTON MCKENNIE

"Once you get in that game mode, you just are out there competing, and that's all that really matters."

— *Weston McKennie*

Who is Weston McKennie?

Have you heard about Weston McKennie? He's super amazing! McKennie is an awesome soccer player who plays for Juventus and the US Men's National Team. He's like a soccer superstar, and he's only 25 years old! Can you believe it?

So, get this, McKennie's soccer journey started when he was just a little kid. He was born in the USA, but then his family moved to Germany because his dad was in the army. How cool is that? While living in Germany, McKennie fell in love with soccer. He started playing when he was really young, like maybe six years old! And guess what? He got really, really good at it.

When he was a bit older, McKennie moved back to the USA and joined the FC Dallas Academy. That's where he honed his skills and showed everyone how talented he was. He even won some big championships with them! But McKennie's dreams were bigger than just playing in the USA. He wanted to play in Europe, where the best soccer teams are.

And guess what? He made it happen! McKennie moved to Germany to play for Schalke, a famous soccer team. He was so good that he caught the attention of Juventus, one of the biggest teams in Italy. Can you imagine playing for Juventus? It's a dream come true!

But wait, there's more! McKennie doesn't just play for his club team, he also plays for the US Men's National Team. He's like a hero for his country! He's scored amazing goals, won big tournaments, and was even named "Player of the Tournament!" How awesome is that?

Off the field, McKennie is also really cool. He speaks different languages and loves Harry Potter. Isn't that neat? Oh, and did I mention he can play the piano too? He's like a real-life superhero!

So, yeah, Weston McKennie is basically the coolest soccer player ever. He's living his dream, making his country proud, and showing everyone that with hard work and dedication, anything is possible! Go McKennie!

The American Engine

Weston McKennie was a super talented kid with big dreams of playing soccer all over the world. Everyone said he was the "American Engine" because he was an energetic and creative midfielder and was going to be a leading force in making American soccer really awesome on the world stage.

One day, McKennie was practicing soccer with his friends at the park. "Hey McKennie, why do you think you'll be so good at soccer?" his friend Billy asked.

"Well, Billy," McKennie replied with a big smile, "I love playing soccer more than anything else in the world! And I work really, really hard every single day to get better."

"Yeah, but lots of people love soccer. What makes you so special?" Billy wondered.

"I think it's because I never give up, no matter what," McKennie explained. "Even when things get tough, I keep trying my best and learning from my mistakes. And I always encourage my teammates to do the same!"

"Wow, McKennie, you're like a superhero!" Billy exclaimed.

McKennie laughed. "I don't know about that, but I do know that I want to make my country proud. I want to show everyone that American soccer players can be just as good as anyone else in the world!"

And so, with his passion, determination, and a little bit of magic, Weston McKennie continued to chase his dreams of becoming a soccer superstar. And everyone believed that he would indeed be a leading force in propelling American soccer onto the world stage.

Breaking Barriers

McKennie used to live in Germany when he was a little kid, where he played soccer with his friends. It was so much fun! He was born in Texas, but his father, a United States Air Force officer, was stationed at nearby Ramstein Air Base.

When he was in Germany, McKennie played soccer, and he was really, really good at it. He practiced all the time, and he never gave up on his dreams. One day, McKennie said to his mom, "Mom, I want to be a soccer star someday!"

His mom smiled and said, "You can do it! Just keep working hard and believing in yourself."

And guess what? McKennie did it! He worked super hard, and he got really good at soccer. Then one day, he got a big chance to play soccer for a really famous team!

When McKennie got the call, he couldn't believe it! He was going to play for a big team! Putting on his new jersey felt like wearing a superhero cape. He knew he was going to do amazing things!

But McKennie's journey wasn't just about soccer. He became a hero for lots of kids who loved soccer, just like him. He showed them that if you work hard and never give up, you can make your dreams come true, too!

Off the field, McKennie did even more amazing stuff. He helped other kids learn to play soccer and shared his secrets to success. He wanted everyone to know that with practice and believing in yourself, anything is possible!

So, Weston McKennie became not just a soccer star, but also a hero for kids everywhere. His story reminds us all to dream big and never, ever give up!

The Future of US Soccer

Weston McKennie is like the superhero of soccer for the US Men's National Team! Lots of people think he's super special and will help American soccer become really, really awesome around the world. Here's why…

McKennie can do lots of cool stuff on the soccer field! It's like he has magic soccer powers because he can play in different places, like running all over as a midfielder or helping out the defense when they need him. And guess what? He's super good at it!

But that's not all! McKennie is also really, really good with the ball. He can dribble past defenders with godlike ease, pass the ball to his teammates with perfect accuracy, and even kick it into the net to score goals! It's like he's playing a video game, but in real life!

And he's not just good at soccer stuff. McKennie is also super strong and fast! He can run around the field for a long time without getting tired and jump really high to get the ball in the air. Plus, he's always cheering on his teammates and telling them what to do, just like a team captain!

But you know what's even cooler? McKennie has traveled all around the world playing soccer! He's been to places like Italy, where he played for a famous team called Juventus. That's like being a soccer superhero in different countries!

And guess what? Kids all over America look up to McKennie. They see him playing on TV and think, "Wow, I want to be just like him when I grow up!" He's like a big brother showing everyone that if you work hard and believe in yourself, you can do anything… even become a soccer superstar like him!

So, Weston McKennie is not just a soccer player. He's a hero who's helping American soccer become the best it can be! Go, McKennie!

Weston McKennie Reflection Questions

1. Have you ever dreamed of being a soccer superstar like Weston McKennie? What do you think makes him so cool?

2. If you could ask Weston McKennie one question about soccer, what would it be? Why do you want to know that?

CHAPTER 16

HOPE SOLO

"There are no shortcuts. If you feel good, you'll look good, you'll play good. Work hard every day. No matter what your strengths and weaknesses, there's no substitute for hard work."

-Hope Solo

Who is Hope Solo?

Have you heard about Hope Solo? She's an amazing soccer player who has done so many cool things! Let me tell you all about her!

Hope Solo was born on July 30, 1981, in a place called Richland, Washington. When she was little, she played soccer as a forward and scored a whopping 109 goals for her high school team! She was so good that she was named an All-American by Parade Magazine, twice! That's a big deal!

After high school, Hope went to the University of Washington, where she switched from being a forward to a goalkeeper. And guess what? She was fantastic at it! She became a star player for the Washington Huskies and was named an All-American three times. She even won a special award called the Hermann Award in her senior year for being so awesome!

In 2004, Hope was picked as an alternate for the U.S. Olympic Team, but she didn't get to play in the Athens games. That didn't stop her, though. By 2005, she became the top goalkeeper for the U.S. Women's National Team, playing 1,054 minutes without letting a single goal get past her! Can you believe that?

Then, in 2008, something incredible happened. Hope helped the U.S. team win a gold medal at the Summer Olympics in Beijing! Four years later, at the London Olympics, she did it again, helping her team win another gold medal! And in 2015, she was a superstar at the FIFA Women's World Cup, where the U.S. team won the championship. Hope was so good that she won the

Golden Glove Award twice, in 2011 and 2015, for being the best goalkeeper.

Hope's journey wasn't always easy, though. In 2007, she was benched during a big game against Brazil in the World Cup, and she was really upset about it. She spoke out, and it caused some trouble, but she came back stronger than ever. Even when things got tough, like when she was suspended in 2016, Hope never gave up. She even fought for equal pay for female soccer players and became a commentator for the BBC during the 2019 World Cup.

Through all the ups and downs, Hope Solo has been an incredible athlete and an inspiration to so many people. She's shown that with hard work and determination, you can achieve amazing things!

The Fearless Leader

Hope Solo is known far and wide as a legendary goalkeeper. When she's guarding the goal, it's like she has a force field around it! She's quick, agile, and fearless, making it super hard for the other team to score.

But that's not all there is to Hope Solo. She's also famous for her outspoken personality. She's not afraid to speak up and say what she thinks, on and off the field. Whether it's about soccer or important issues like fairness and equality, she never hesitates to share her thoughts.

And when it comes to stopping shots, Hope Solo is simply incredible. She's like a superhero with super reflexes, diving and jumping to block shots that seem impossible to stop. Her shot-stopping abilities have earned her the admiration of fans all over the world.

But perhaps what makes Hope Solo even more amazing is her advocacy for women's equality. She's a fierce advocate for making sure everyone, regardless of gender, gets treated fairly and equally in soccer. Through her actions and words, she's breaking down barriers and inspiring others to fight for what's right.

A Trailblazer for Goalkeepers

Did you know that Hope Solo's career seriously redefined the goalkeeper position in women's soccer?

Her insane skills and performances on the field raised the bar for goalkeeping in the women's game. Solo's agility, reflexes, and strong presence in the goal made her a scary opponent for any team. Her ability to make crazy saves in high-pressure situations set a new standard for what it means to win as a goalkeeper.

Additionally, Solo's success helped change how everyone thought of the goalkeeper's role. Lots of people used to see this as a defensive position primarily focused on stopping goals, but Solo showed us that goalkeepers can also play a very important role in starting attacks and helping out with their team's offensive play. Her skillful distribution and ability to start counterattacks with very on-point long passes showed everyone the importance of a goalkeeper's role in building attacks from the back.

CHAPTER 16: HOPE SOLO

Even when things got tough, like when she had to face really tough opponents or deal with unfair stuff, she never gave up. Solo showed everyone that girls can be amazing goalkeepers! And she didn't just play soccer... she also talked about important stuff like making sure girls get treated the same as boys. Her willingness to speak out on issues such as gender equality and equal pay also helped to make the profile of women's soccer even better and bring attention to important issues within the sport.

Overall, Hope Solo's career not only raised the bar for goalkeeping awesomeness, but also helped to rethink the role of the goalkeeper in women's soccer, showing us all the importance of both defensive prowess and offensive contribution.

More Than Just a Game

Hope Solo didn't just play soccer; she also used her voice to speak up for important things like fairness and equality. In 2016, she spoke out against unfair treatment in soccer and fought for equal pay for women players. She even filed a lawsuit against U.S. Soccer to demand equal pay for women players like herself.

That's not all; in March 2016, she joined hands with some of her teammates and complained about getting paid less than male soccer players even though they worked just as hard.

She didn't stop there; in 2018, she took it a step further by filing a federal lawsuit against U.S. Soccer, asking them to pay female players the same as male players.

Hope Solo wasn't just a soccer star; she was also a champion for women's rights, inspiring young athletes everywhere to stand up for fairness and equality.

Hope Solo Reflection Questions

1. What do you think makes Hope Solo a special soccer player?

2. How do you think Hope Solo's determination and resilience helped her overcome challenges in her soccer career?

3. Why do you think it's important for athletes like Hope Solo to speak up for what they believe in, on and off the field?

CHAPTER 17

ROBERTO CARLOS

"Remember to always smile."

-*Roberto Carlos*

Who is Roberto Carlos?

Let me tell you all about Roberto Carlos! He's not just any soccer player; he's a LEGEND! Roberto Carlos was born on April 10, 1973, in Garça, Sao Paulo, Brazil. But get this, his childhood wasn't all sunshine and rainbows. Nope, he grew up in poverty, working in a textile factory at just 12 years old to help his family. Can you imagine?

But wait, here's where it gets super cool! Despite all the tough stuff, Roberto never gave up on his dream of becoming a soccer star. He played soccer whenever he could, and all that hard work paid off big time!

Roberto started his professional career with Uniao Sao Joao in Sao Paulo. Then, in 1992, he moved to Atletico Mineiro. But that's not all! He joined Palmeiras in 1993 and then Inter Milan in 1995. But here's the kicker: In 1996, he made a BIG move to Real Madrid! Can you believe it? Real Madrid! He played there until 2007, making history with his powerful strikes and lightning speed. Oh, and he even wore the famous number 3 jersey!

But wait, there's more! After his time in Madrid, he played for Fenerbahce, Corinthians, and Anzhi Makhachkala. And even tried his hand at coaching! From Anzhi Makhachkala to Sivasspor, Akhisarspor, and Delhi Dynamos, Roberto showed that he's not just a star player; he's a star coach too!

But here's the best part: Roberto has done so much charity work, like playing in Soccer Aid and becoming a global ambassador for Football for Friendship. He's not just a legend on the field; he's a legend off the field too!

So there you have it, folks! Roberto Carlos isn't just a soccer player; he's a hero, a record-breaker, and a true inspiration!

The King of the Free Kick

Roberto Carlos is famous for his amazing kicks, especially free kicks. One day, during a big game between Brazil and France, Roberto had a chance to show off his skills.

It was a warm summer's day in 1997, and the stage was set for an epic showdown between Brazil and France in Le Tournoi. The crowd was insanely loud as the two soccer giants prepared to clash on the hallowed turf.

As the match went on, tensions ran high. Both teams fought tooth and nail, each battling to be the best on the field. But then, in the 21st minute, fate came into play, and the course of soccer history would be forever changed!

Brazil was awarded a free kick, a precious opportunity to seize the advantage. And who better to take it than the maestro himself, Roberto Carlos?

Roberto stood far from the goal, looking at the ball. With a big run-up, he kicked the ball with all his might. Everyone watched as the ball flew through the air. But here's the crazy part: the ball seemed to go the wrong way at first, but then it curved back and went into the goal!

People couldn't believe their eyes. How did he do that? It was like magic! Roberto's kick was so powerful and precise that it confused everyone, even the goalkeeper. He scored goals like this many times, from really far away or from strange angles.

Fans loved watching Roberto play because they never knew what amazing thing he would do next. His free kick was just one example of his incredible talent and technique. It's no wonder he became a legend in the world of soccer!

An Attacking Force from Defense

Roberto Carlos wasn't your typical defender; he was a force to be reckoned with going forward as well. His style of play revolutionized the role of the full-back, bringing a new dimension to the game with his attacking prowess.

One of his trademark moves was the overlapping run. Instead of staying back in defense, Roberto would charge forward, overlapping with his teammates to provide an extra option in attack. His blistering speed and stamina allowed him to cover ground quickly, often catching opposing defenses off guard.

But it wasn't just his speed that made him dangerous; it was also his pinpoint crosses. Roberto had the ability to whip in crosses with incredible accuracy, delivering the ball right onto the head or foot of his teammates in the box. This made him a valuable asset during set-piece situations and open play, as his crosses created numerous goal-scoring opportunities for his team.

And let's not forget about his contributions to his team's offense. Despite being a defender, Roberto was never afraid to take on defenders and create scoring chances for himself. His powerful shots from a distance and his ability to dribble past opponents made him a constant threat in the attacking third of the pitch.

Overall, Roberto Carlos was much more than just a defensive stalwart. He was a dynamic player who played a crucial role in his team's offense, thanks to his overlapping runs, pinpoint crosses, and fearless approach to attacking play.

A Legacy of Excitement

Roberto Carlos's attacking style and explosive free kicks didn't just entertain fans; they inspired a whole generation of young players to embrace the attacking side of the game from the defense.

His fearless approach to the game showed young defenders that they didn't have to just focus on stopping the opposition; they could also contribute to their team's attack. Roberto's overlapping runs and willingness to push forward encouraged defenders to be more adventurous and creative with their play.

But it was his free kicks that truly captured the imagination of aspiring soccer players around the world. Roberto's ability to bend the ball in ways that seemed impossible inspired countless youngsters to practice their own set-piece techniques. Whether it was curling shots around the wall or blasting the ball with power, young players tried to emulate Roberto's iconic free kicks on playgrounds and training grounds everywhere.

His influence extended beyond just his playing style; Roberto's success showed young defenders that they could be more than just stoppers. They could be playmakers, goal scorers, and game changers. His legacy lives on in the attacking full-backs of today, who continue to push forward and make their mark on the game, just like Roberto Carlos did in his prime.

Roberto Carlos Reflection Questions

1. How do you think Roberto Carlos balanced his defensive responsibilities with his attacking flair?

2. How do you think Roberto Carlos's background and upbringing influenced his playing style and mentality on the field?

3. What do you think drove Roberto Carlos to continue playing at the highest level for so many years?

CHAPTER 18

GIANLUIGI BUFFON

"I believe in doing the right things; that is my character and personality."

-Gianluigi Buffon

Who is Gianluigi Buffon?

Gianluigi Buffon, also known as Gigi Buffon, was born on January 28, 1978, in Carrara, Italy. Wow, that's a long time ago! But he's still super famous today! His family was super sporty too! His mom was a champion in shot put and discus throw, and his dad and sisters were into sports too!

When Buffon was just a little kid, he loved playing soccer with his friends. He was so good that he joined the Parma youth team when he was only 13 years old! Can you imagine being that talented at such a young age?

But guess what? Buffon didn't start off as a goalkeeper! Nope, he played in different positions before he realized he was meant to be a goalie. He was inspired by a famous goalkeeper named Thomas N'Kono, who played for Cameroon in the World Cup. And guess what else? Buffon made his Serie A debut for Parma when he was just 17 years old! That's so young!

He played for Parma for a while, winning lots of cool trophies like the UEFA Cup and the Coppa Italia. Then, in 2001, Buffon joined Juventus for a record-breaking fee! He became their star goalkeeper and won so many Serie A titles with them! He was like a wall, stopping all the shots that came his way!

Buffon was also a superhero for Italy's national team! He played in five FIFA World Cup tournaments and even won the 2006 World Cup! Can you imagine lifting that big trophy up in the air with all your teammates cheering?

But Buffon wasn't just famous for his goalkeeping skills. He was also a super nice guy and a great leader on and off the field. He inspired so many young players to work hard and follow their dreams.

After playing for Juventus and shortly for Paris Saint-Germain, Buffon went back to his first club, Parma, before retiring in 2023. But even though he's not playing anymore, people still talk about him all the time! He's a soccer legend, and everyone will remember him forever!

Gianluigi Buffon was not just a goalkeeper; he was a real-life superhero who showed us that with hard work and determination, you can achieve anything!

The Wall of Italy

Picture this: the ball is flying towards the goal like a speeding bullet, and everyone in the stadium is holding their breath. But then, out of nowhere, Buffon leaps into action, diving through the air like a majestic eagle, stretching his arms out as far as they can go!

With lightning-fast reflexes, he blocks the ball from entering the net, making it look like child's play. He's like a real-life superhero, saving the day one dive at a time!

But what makes Buffon's diving saves so incredible? It's not just his lightning-fast reflexes, although those are definitely impressive. It's also his incredible anticipation and positioning.

He always seems to know exactly where the ball will go before it leaves the opponent's foot!

For this and many other reasons, Buffon's name is synonymous with "greatness!" He's like a shield, protecting his team's goal with lightning-fast reflexes and fearless dives. What's really amazing is how he's been doing this for so many years and is still at the top of his game. He's not just a goalie; he's a living legend who proves that with passion and dedication, you can achieve greatness.

A Leader by Example

"We need you, Gigi."

It was the final moments of the match, tension thick in the air like a fog. Gianluigi Buffon, the iconic goalkeeper, looked around at his teammates, who were huddled around him, seemingly on edge. But Buffon stood firm at the goal post, his eyes fixed on the ball as if it held the secrets of victory.

Buffon flashed a reassuring smile.

"Trust me, guys. I've got this," he replied, his voice steady as a rock.

The opponents launched a blistering attack, the ball hurtling towards the net like a missile. Buffon sprang into action, his body a blur of motion as he dove with lightning speed, fingertips grazing the ball in a crazy-wild save.

The stadium erupted into thunderous applause, but Buffon remained unfazed, his focus unwavering.

"That's why they call me the Wall," he joked to everyone.

His teammates exchanged knowing looks, confidence bursting like fireworks. With Buffon guarding the goal, they knew anything was possible.

In moments like these, Buffon's leadership shone brightest. He was not just a goalkeeper; he was a pillar of strength, guiding his team to victory with skill, determination, and unwavering belief.

A Legend Leaves His Mark

On a bright afternoon, a young goalkeeper sat mesmerized in front of the TV, watching Gianluigi Buffon make yet another miraculous save.

"Wow, did you see that?" he exclaimed to his father, who nodded with a smile. "He's incredible," the father replied.

Years flew by, and that once-young goalkeeper honed his skills tirelessly, fueled by the memory of Buffon's heroics.

"I want to be like him one day," he told his coach, determination gleaming in his eyes.

Finally, the moment arrived. Standing on the field where Buffon once stood, the goalkeeper took a deep breath.

"This is it," he whispered to himself, feeling the weight of his hero's legacy on his shoulders.

As the final whistle blew, the crowd erupted into cheers, and the goalkeeper's heart swelled with pride.

"Thank you, Buffon," he whispered, knowing that he owed his success to the inspiration of a legend.

Gianluigi Buffon's career may have ended, but his spirit lives on in every goalkeeper who dares to dream big and reach for greatness.

You see, Gianluigi Buffon played soccer for a really long time - more than twenty years! He was super good at stopping goals and became really famous in the sport. People loved him for his skills and also because he was a nice guy.

He played for teams like Parma and Juventus, winning lots of trophies and setting records along the way. But what's even cooler is how he inspired other goalkeepers. Buffon showed them that if you work hard and never give up, you can achieve anything.

So, even though Buffon retired, his legacy lives on. He's a role model for young goalkeepers, showing them that they can reach for the stars and chase their dreams, just like he did.

Gianluigi Buffon Reflection Questions

1. How do you think Buffon inspired other players with his skills and personality?

2. Why do you think Buffon is considered one of the greatest goalkeepers of all time?

3. What do you think Buffon's legacy will be in the world of soccer?

CHAPTER 19

ALPHONSO DAVIES

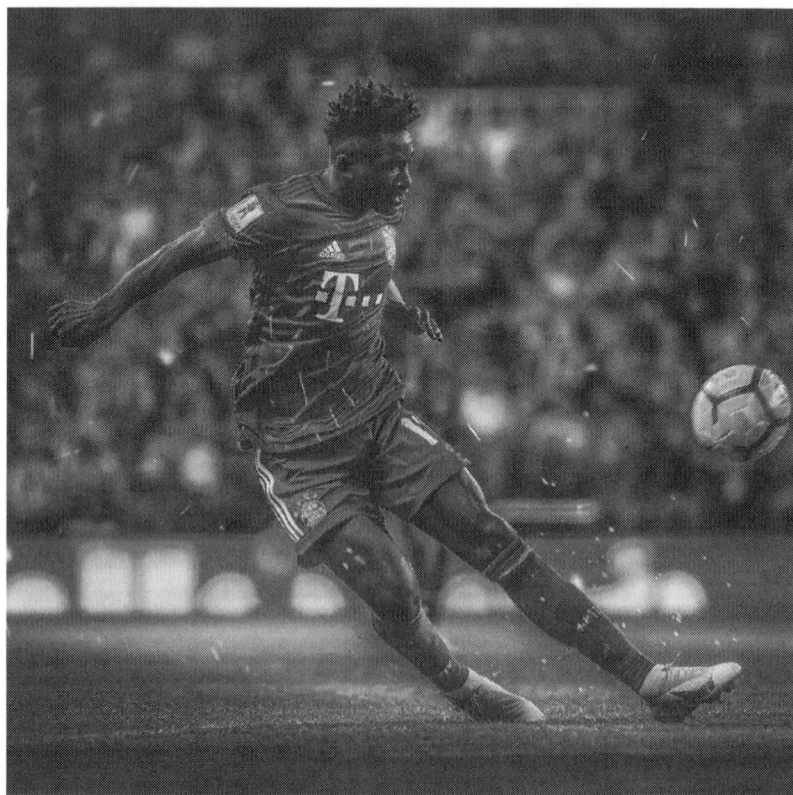

"Don't give up, no matter how hard it is. Things are going to be tough down the road, but the more work you put in, the more achievement you're going to get out of it."

-Alphonso Davies

Who is Alphonso Davies?

In a faraway place called Buduburam, Ghana, there lived a little boy named Alphonso Davies. He wasn't just any ordinary kid; he was born on November 2, 2000, and his story is a thrilling roller coaster ride!

Alphonso's journey began in a refugee camp, where he played soccer with his siblings, dreaming of becoming a soccer superstar. But life had big plans for him! When he was just five years old, his family moved to Canada, seeking a better life. Little did they know, they were nurturing a future soccer sensation!

As Alphonso grew up in Edmonton, soccer became his passion. He joined the Edmonton Internationals and later the Edmonton Strikers, showing off his skills on the field. But it was his move to Vancouver at the age of 14 that changed everything. There, he joined the Whitecaps FC Residency program, where his talent truly shone like a shooting star!

In 2016, at the tender age of 15, Alphonso signed with Whitecaps FC 2, becoming the youngest player in the USL! He made headlines by scoring his first professional goal at just 15 years and 6 months old – talk about a prodigy!

But Alphonso's story was just beginning. He quickly rose through the ranks, catching the attention of European giants like Bayern Munich. In 2018, Bayern made a multi-million-dollar transfer offer, and Alphonso waved goodbye to Vancouver, ready to conquer the soccer world!

His debut with Bayern was like a dream come true — a whirlwind of excitement! From scoring his first Bundesliga goal to winning multiple league titles and even the UEFA Champions League, Alphonso's career skyrocketed faster than a speeding bullet!

But Alphonso isn't just a soccer star; he's a hero off the pitch too! As an ambassador for the UN refugee agency, he's using his fame to make the world a better place — a real-life superhero!

From his humble beginnings in Ghana to becoming one of the best full-backs in the world, Alphonso Davies' story is a true fairy tale. And who knows what adventures await this young soccer wizard in the years to come? The sky's the limit for Alphonso — or should I say, the stars!

The Bayern Bullet

Did you know that Alphonso Davies is faster than a cheetah chasing its dinner? It's true! This soccer superstar can zoom across the field faster than you can say "super speed!"

Alphonso Davies isn't just your average full-back — he's a dynamo of energy, a whirlwind of speed tearing up the field like a comet streaking across the sky! He leaves defenders in his dust and sends shivers down the spines of opposing teams.

Once, during a game against Werder Bremen, Alphonso reached a mind-blowing speed of 36.51 kilometers per hour! Can you imagine running that fast? It's like lightning flashing across the sky!

But wait, there's more! When he faced off against Erling Haaland from Borussia Dortmund, Alphonso raced after him at an unbelievable speed of 35.3 kilometers per hour! It was like watching a superhero chase down a villain in a movie!

And get this: Alphonso holds the record for the fastest speed ever clocked in the Bundesliga! He's like the Flash of soccer, leaving defenders in the dust with his lightning-fast moves!

With legs that move faster than a rocket ship blasting off into space, Alphonso Davies is not just a soccer player – he's a speedster extraordinaire!

But it's not just his speed that's impressive; it's the way he uses it to terrorize opposing teams down the flank. Like a whirlwind, he storms past defenders, weaving through challenges with the grace of a dancer and the power of a hurricane.

And when he reaches the opponent's goal, watch out! With lightning-fast footwork and lightning-quick reactions, he slices through defenses like a hot knife through butter, delivering crosses and setting up goals with pinpoint precision.

In every game he plays, Alphonso Davies brings an electrifying energy that sparks excitement and ignites passion in fans around the world. So, next time you see him on the field, buckle up and get ready for a thrilling ride because with Alphonso, anything is possible!

From Refugee Camp to Global Star

In a remarkable rise from a refugee camp to a star player for one of the biggest clubs in the world, Alphonso Davies' journey was nothing short of extraordinary.

As a young boy, Alphonso's family fled the Second Liberian Civil War, seeking refuge in a camp in Ghana. Years later, they found themselves in Canada, where Alphonso's love for soccer blossomed.

"It wasn't easy," Alphonso said. "But soccer was my favorite thing to do."

He was really good at soccer, and people noticed. He got a chance to join the Vancouver Whitecaps FC team, and that's where everything changed.

"I remember watching him play for the first time," his coach said. "He was so special. You could see it right away."

From there, Alphonso's star only continued to rise. His blistering pace and mad skills caught the attention of top clubs around the world, ultimately leading to a historic transfer to Bayern Munich.

"It's like a dream come true," Alphonso cheered, his eyes shining with excitement. "To go from where I started to playing for Bayern, it's beyond anything I could have imagined."

And as he stepped onto the pitch for his first match with Bayern Munich, Alphonso knew that his journey was just beginning. With each sprint down the field and every goal scored, he was not just representing himself, he was representing every young dreamer with a passion for the beautiful game.

A Beacon of Hope

Alphonso Davies isn't just a soccer star; he also inspires lots of kids all over the world. Even though he's really famous now, he doesn't forget where he came from. He grew up in a tough situation, but he never gave up on his dream of playing soccer.

Alphonso likes to share his story to show other kids that they can do amazing things too, no matter where they're from. He talks about how soccer helped him when he was going through hard times and how it became his favorite thing to do. He wants kids to know that if they work hard and believe in themselves, they can also make their dreams come true.

He's also really friendly and likes to chat with his fans online. He answers their questions and shares messages of encouragement. By doing this, he makes kids feel like they're important and that they can achieve anything they set their minds to.

Alphonso also helps out with charities that help kids who don't have as many opportunities. He gives his time and money to groups that help kids play sports and go to school. He wants to make sure that every kid has a chance to follow their dreams, just like he did.

Alphonso Davies is like a big brother to kids all over the world, showing them that with hard work and determination, they can do anything they want, no matter where they're from.

Alphonso Davies Reflection Questions

1. How does Alphonso Davies' story motivate you to pursue your own dreams and goals?

2. What can we learn from Alphonso Davies' journey and success?

CHAPTER 20

ABBY WAMBACH

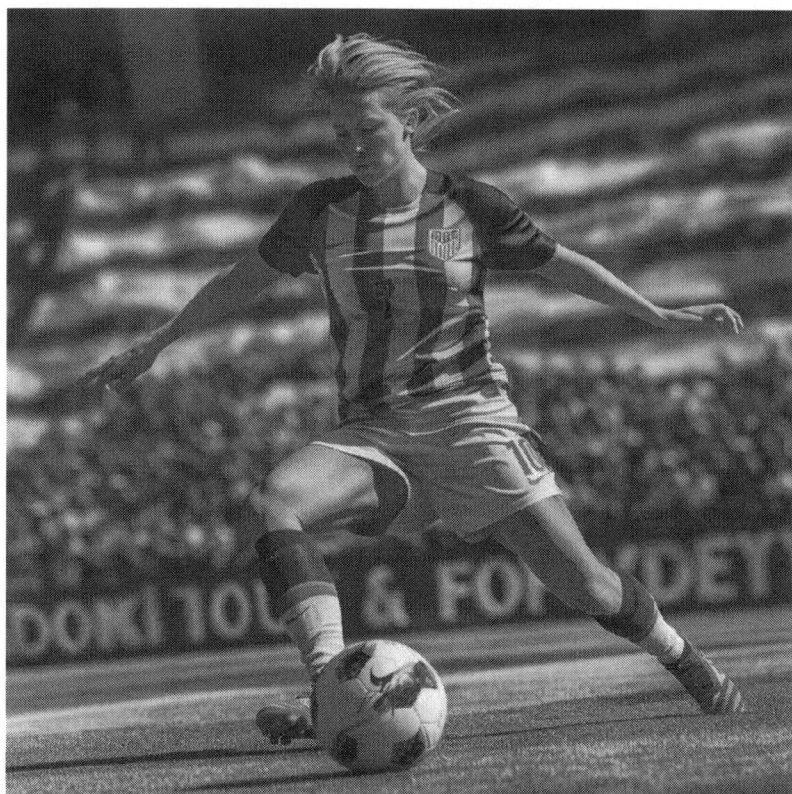

"Don't give up, no matter how hard it is. Things are going to be tough down the road, but the more work you put in, the more achievement you're going to get out of it."

-Abby Wambach

Who is Abby Wambach?

This super-duper amazing soccer player named Abby Wambach was born on June 2, 1980, in Pittsford, New York. That's a looong time ago, even before some of your parents were born!

Abby's love for soccer started when she was just a tiny tot, barely able to walk. At only four years old, she joined soccer leagues and WOWED everyone with her mad skills. Can you imagine? By the time she was a kid, she was already scoring goals like it was nobody's business!

But get this: Abby wasn't just a soccer star. Nope, she was a total sports all-star! She even played basketball in high school and was SO good that she started for FOUR WHOLE YEARS! Can you picture teen Abby dribbling that basketball down the court? What a champ!

Then came college, where Abby rocked the soccer field for the University of Florida Gators. In 1998, she helped lead her team to the NCAA Final Four. That's like the Superbowl of college soccer, folks!

Fast forward to 2002 – Abby's big break! She got drafted as the second pick in the Women's United Soccer Association (WUSA) draft. That's like getting picked first for your dream team on the playground!

Abby's soccer journey took her to the big leagues, winning gold medals at the 2004 and 2012 Olympics. She even scored her

100th international goal in 2009 – talk about a GOAL-SCORING MACHINE!

But wait, there's more! In 2011, Abby was named the Associated Press Female Athlete of the Year. She was also FIFA World Player of the Year in 2012 – the BEST of the BEST!

And get this, friends... Abby wasn't just amazing on the field. Nope, she's a hero off the field too! She became an ambassador for Athlete Ally in 2013, standing up for equality and fairness in sports. What a champion!

So, there you have it, the incredible journey of Abby Wambach, from a tiny tot kicking soccer balls to a superstar champion on and off the field!

The Warrior on the Field

Abby Wambach is hailed as a true warrior on the field, and for good reason! She's not just a soccer player; she's a force to be reckoned with, a legend in her own right. With two Olympic gold medals under her belt, Abby has proven time and time again that she's one of the greatest forwards to ever grace the game.

What sets Abby apart is her relentless work ethic. Picture her on the field, giving her all in every training session, every match, every single moment. She doesn't know the meaning of "taking it easy" – she's always pushing herself to be better, stronger, and faster.

And let's talk about her iconic header; it's like a thunderbolt on the field! Abby's aerial prowess is unmatched, striking fear into the hearts of defenders and leaving goalkeepers scrambling to stop her powerful shots. She's a master of the air, dominating the game with her towering presence and pinpoint accuracy.

But Abby's greatness goes beyond her skills on the field. She's a born leader, unafraid to speak her mind and rally her teammates to victory. Her voice echoes across the pitch, inspiring those around her to give their all and never back down from a challenge.

And that's what makes Abby Wambach a true warrior – her dedication to the sport, her incredible goal-scoring record, and her never-give-up attitude. She's a shining example of what it means to chase your dreams with all your heart, and her legacy will inspire generations of athletes to come.

A Champion for Equality

Abby Wambach wasn't just a soccer superstar; she was also a fierce advocate for equality in women's sports. Throughout her career, Abby used her platform to shine a spotlight on the disparities between men's and women's athletics, particularly when it came to pay and opportunities.

She wasn't afraid to speak out against unfairness, boldly calling for equal pay for female athletes who poured their hearts and souls into their sport just like their male counterparts. Abby knew that women athletes need to be treated with the same respect as male athletes, and she fought tirelessly to make that a reality.

Her words were not just talk – she took action. Abby worked with organizations dedicated to promoting gender equality in sports, using her voice to strengthen the voices of those fighting for change. She lobbied for policy changes and worked to raise awareness about the importance of equal pay and opportunities for female athletes.

Abby's impact goes far beyond the soccer field. Her efforts paved the way for future' generations of female athletes, inspiring them to stand up for their rights and demand the recognition they deserve. Thanks to Abby's hard work, the landscape of women's sports is changing for the better, and her legacy will continue to inspire generations to come.

Inspiring the Next Generation

Abby Wambach isn't just a soccer star; she's a mentor and a champion for young athletes worldwide. Through her motivational speeches, she ignites a fire within kids, inspiring them to believe in themselves and go after their goals with all their hearts. Abby's passion for empowering youth extends beyond words. She actively engages in youth programs, where she not only teaches soccer skills but also imparts valuable life lessons about teamwork, resilience, and leadership.

One of the youth programs Abby is involved in is the "Abby Wambach Soccer Academy," where she shares her expertise with budding soccer players. In these sessions, she not only focuses on improving their game but also emphasizes the importance of determination, discipline, and self-belief. Through her personal experiences, she shows them that success doesn't come easy, but with dedication and perseverance, they can overcome any challenge.

Moreover, Abby's dedication to empowering young girls goes beyond the soccer field. She advocates for gender equality in sports, ensuring that girls have the same opportunities as boys to pursue their athletic dreams. By breaking down barriers and challenging stereotypes, Abby encourages girls to step onto the field with confidence, knowing that their voices matter and their dreams are valid.

Abby's impact on the next generation of athletes is immeasurable. She's not just teaching them how to play soccer; she's instilling in them the belief that they can achieve greatness both on and off the field. Through her actions and words, she's building a legacy of empowerment, one young athlete at a time.

Abby Wambach Reflection Questions

1. How do you think Abby's experiences as a soccer player have shaped her as a person?

2. What do you think kids can do to follow in Abby's footsteps and make a positive impact in their own communities?

```

```

3. What does it mean to be a "warrior" like Abby Wambach?

```

```

CHAPTER 21

MICHELLE AKERS

"I think the challenge is to take difficult and painful times and turn them into something beneficial, something that makes you grow."

-Michelle Akers

Who is Michelle Akers?

Oh wow, let me tell you about the amazing Michelle Akers! She's like a real-life superhero! Michelle was born on February 1, 1966, in Santa Clara, California. Can you believe she wanted to play football for the Pittsburgh Steelers when she was little? But her teacher said, "Girls don't play football." So, guess what? Michelle found soccer instead, and she was super awesome at it!

When she was growing up in Seattle, Michelle was like a soccer wizard. She went to Shorecrest High School and became a three-time All-American! She was so good that she got to play for the U.S. national team for the first time in 1985. I wasn't even born then!

Then Michelle went to the University of Central Florida, and she was a superstar there too. She was a four-time All-American and won the very first Hermann Trophy in 1988 for being the best college soccer player in the country! How cool is that?

Michelle's soccer career just kept getting more amazing. In 1991, she played in the first-ever Women's World Cup in China and scored 10 goals! She helped the U.S. win the World Cup, and she scored the winning goal in the final game. Talk about clutch!

But Michelle's journey wasn't always easy. In 1991, she started feeling really tired all the time and found out she had chronic fatigue immune dysfunction syndrome (CFIDS). Even though it made things super hard, Michelle didn't give up. She kept playing and even won a gold medal at the 1996 Olympics in Atlanta. She was like a soccer warrior!

And then, in 1999, Michelle and her team won the World Cup again! This time, it was in Pasadena, California, and it was so hot, like 110 degrees on the field. Michelle played her heart out until she couldn't stand anymore. The team won in a dramatic shootout, and everyone was cheering like crazy!

After all those amazing soccer adventures, Michelle retired in 2000. But she didn't stop being awesome. She trained to become a physician's assistant and worked with the women's national team doctor. She also created a sports ministry called Soccer Outreach International to help others.

Michelle Akers is a true legend, a champion on and off the field, and her story is one of never giving up no matter what. She's my hero, and I think she's the coolest soccer player ever!

A Pioneer of the Women's Game

Michelle Akers was an amazing soccer player who played as a forward and dominated the women's game in the early 1990s. She had incredible skills, like powerful shooting and great ball control, which made her a tough opponent. Michelle was also very strong and could snag headers from defenders easily. She was smart on the field and knew how to create chances for her team.

Beyond her skills, Michelle was a great leader. Her teammates admired her and looked up to her for inspiration. Even when she was dealing with a serious illness called chronic fatigue immune dysfunction syndrome (CFIDS), she never gave up and always gave her best. This showed her incredible determination and strength.

Michelle's leadership was evident in important games, like the 1991 Women's World Cup, where she scored ten goals and helped the U.S. team win the championship. Her performance in that tournament not only highlighted her talent but also showed how she could bring out the best in her teammates.

She also inspired many young girls to play soccer. At a time when women's sports didn't get much attention, Michelle showed that women could be just as great as men in sports. Her success encouraged future stars like Mia Hamm and Alex Morgan to pursue their dreams.

Even after retiring, Michelle continued to help and inspire others through her sports ministry, Soccer Outreach International. Her legacy lives on as a trailblazer in women's soccer, and many young players today look up to her as a role model.

Overcoming Adversity

Michelle Akers had an amazing soccer career filled with great achievements and tough challenges. She showed incredible perseverance, resilience, and dedication to the sport.

From the beginning, Michelle was a talented and driven player. While attending University of Central Florida, she earned many awards and became a star. Her skill and determination quickly led her to the U.S. Women's National Team, where she played a key role.

Michelle achieved a lot during her career. In 1991, she scored ten goals in the first Women's World Cup, helping the U.S. team win. This made her a soccer superstar. In 1996, she helped the U.S. team win the gold medal at the Atlanta Olympics. Her talent wasn't just in scoring goals but also in leading and inspiring her teammates.

However, Michelle faced big challenges too. She had many injuries and a serious illness called chronic fatigue immune dysfunction syndrome (CFIDS). These problems could have ended her career, but Michelle's determination and toughness kept her playing. Even when in pain and exhausted, she continued to play at the highest level.

Michelle's toughness was especially clear during the 1999 Women's World Cup. In the hot weather at the Rose Bowl, she played her hardest until she collapsed from exhaustion. Her determination inspired her team and fans everywhere. Even when she was taken off the field, her spirit helped push the team to win the championship.

Michelle Akers' dedication to soccer was strong throughout her career. She trained hard, played with passion, and didn't let setbacks stop her. Her legacy is more than just her wins and goals. She showed the world the power of perseverance and resilience, inspiring many young athletes to follow their dreams with the same strong spirit. Her story proves that hard work and determination can lead to greatness.

A Legacy of Excellence

Michelle Akers' contributions to women's soccer are undeniable. Her impact on the game, the awards she earned, and the inspiration she provides to young athletes are truly remarkable.

Michelle played a huge role in making women's soccer popular. Her skill, hard work, and dedication helped the U.S. Women's National Team achieve great success. In 1991, she scored ten goals in the first Women's World Cup, leading the U.S. team to victory. This made her one of the best players in the world. In 1996, she helped the team win a gold medal at the Atlanta Olympics.

Michelle earned many awards during her career. She was named the U.S. Soccer Female Athlete of the Year twice and won the FIFA Women's Player of the Century award in 2000. Her achievements showed the world that women's soccer was exciting and worth watching.

Beyond her awards and victories, Michelle's influence extends to young athletes everywhere. She showed that with hard work and determination, anything is possible. Even when she faced injuries and a serious illness, she kept playing and never gave up. This resilience inspires young players to keep going, no matter the challenges they face.

Michelle Akers' legacy lives on through the many athletes she has inspired. Her contributions to the growth of women's soccer have paved the way for future generations to succeed and dream big. She proves that dedication and passion can change the world, one goal at a time.

Michelle Akers Reflection Questions

1. What can we learn from Michelle Akers?

2. Why is it important to remember Michelle Akers?

3. How does Akers' story inspire perseverance in soccer?

Chapter "Good Will"

Research has shown that helping others without expecting anything in return can increase happiness and satisfaction in life. In today's reading or listening experience, I would like to give you the opportunity to experience that same feeling. All it requires is a few moments of your time to answer a simple question:

Would you be willing to make a difference in the life of someone you have never met without spending any money or seeking recognition for your good deed?

If your answer is yes, then I have a small request for you. If you have found value in your reading or listening experience today, I humbly ask that you take a brief moment to leave an honest review of this book. It will only take 30 seconds of your time - just a few seconds to share your thoughts with others.

Your feedback can help someone else discover the same inspiration and knowledge that you have gained from this book. If you are unsure of how to leave a review for a Kindle or e-reader book, it is quite simple:

If you have a physical copy of this book, you can find the book page on Amazon (or wherever you purchased it) and leave your review there.

If you are reading on Kindle or an e-reader, simply scroll to the book's last page and swipe up or, <u>click here and find my book</u>

- If you've purchased many items on Amazon after my book, you may need to scroll down a bit!. The review prompt should appear.

Conclusion

Tommy and Sarah sat on the bleachers, watching the other kids play soccer at their school. The sun was shining, and the sound of kids laughing and cheering filled the air.

"Wow, look at them go," Tommy said, eyes wide with admiration. "They're really good!"

Sarah nodded, her eyes following the ball as it zipped across the field. "Yeah, they are. But you know what? After learning about all those amazing soccer stories, I feel like we could do it, too."

Tommy turned to her, curious. "Really? Like whose stories?"

"Like Michelle Akers," Sarah replied, smiling. "She faced so many challenges but never gave up. And Mia Hamm, who worked so hard to become one of the best players ever. They all started just like us, with a dream and a lot of practice."

Tommy grinned. "You're right. It's pretty inspiring. If they could do it, maybe we can too."

Sarah nodded enthusiastically. "Absolutely! This journey through the lives of soccer legends has made me realize that these incredible players weren't born superstars. They started with a dream, worked really hard, and had a burning desire to be the best."

"Yeah," Tommy said, feeling a surge of confidence. "I feel more confident and inspired to give it a try myself. It's all about working hard and never giving up."

"Exactly," Sarah agreed. "Let's remember a few key things: They believed in themselves, practiced a lot, and never let setbacks stop them. If we keep these in mind, who knows? Maybe we'll be the ones inspiring others someday."

Tommy stood up, ready to join the game. "Let's go, Sarah. Let's start our own soccer journey!"

Sarah jumped up beside him, a determined look on her face.

"Let's do it, Tommy! Time to make our dream come true."

And with that, they ran onto the field, ready to chase their soccer dreams.

Just like Tommy and Sarah, lots of kids like you and your friends can feel inspired to follow their dreams by listening to soccer stories. The path to greatness requires dedication, hard work, and the ability to overcome setbacks. We can learn from the legends' relentless pursuit of improvement and their unwavering belief in themselves.

One thing to remember is that soccer is more than just winning; it's about the joy of playing, the thrill of competition, and the creativity expressed on the field. Let these legends inspire you to find your own unique style and passion for the sport.

Don't forget to be a leader and a role model. Through these stories, we can take inspiration from these players who used their platforms to advocate for positive change. Remember, leadership isn't just about skill; it's about inspiring others and making a difference.

Now it's your turn to step onto the field and write your own soccer story. With dedication, passion, and the lessons learned from these legends, you too can achieve greatness. So grab your ball, lace up your cleats, and get ready to unleash your inner soccer champion!

Join the Adventure with "Inspirational Soccer Stories for Kids"

Hey there, champions of tomorrow! I've got something special for you. If you loved the journey we've been on together, then you're in for a treat. The adventure doesn't have to end here—not when there are so many more stories to be told and heroes to meet!

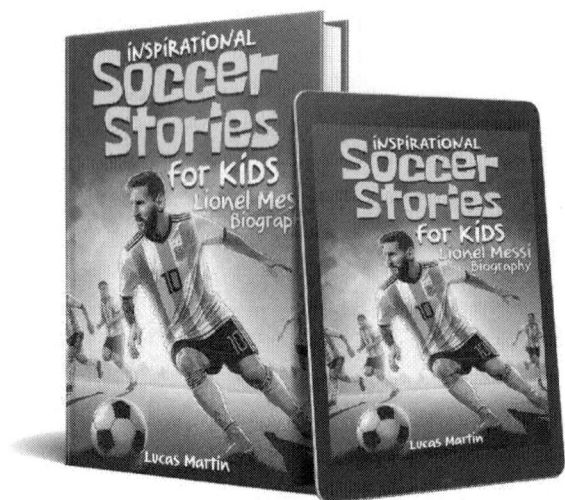

If you're hungry for more tales of triumph, teamwork, and the magic of soccer, then you've got to check out my book series, "Inspirational Soccer Stories for Kids." It's packed with the kind of stories that make you want to lace up your cleats and hit the field, dreaming of your own soccer glory.

And guess what? There's one story that I'm super excited for you to read — **"Inspirational Soccer Stories for Kids: Lionel Messi Biography."** Dive into the life of a boy whose love for soccer took him from the streets of Argentina to the heights of global stardom. It's a tale of determination, passion, and the kind of footwork that'll make your head spin!

So, what are you waiting for? The whistle's blown, and it's time to get the ball rolling. Grab a copy, snuggle up, and get ready to be inspired all over again. Because in the world of soccer, every day is a chance to be inspired, to learn, and to become the legend you're meant to be.

Let's keep the dream alive, team. See you on the next page!

If you want to learn more about Inspirational Soccer Book for Kids and the Soccer Legends, please check out my Author Profile on Amazon here.

Please scan this QR code to access your bonuses

www.sportsstoriesforkids.com/freegift

References

"About." Alex Morgan Foundation, www.alexmorganfoundation.org/about.

"Akers, Michelle." Encyclopedia.com, www.encyclopedia.com/sports/encyclopedias-almanacs-transcripts-and-maps/akers-michelle.

Akers, Michelle. "I Think the Challenge Is to Take Difficult and Painful Times and Turn Them..." QuoteFancy, quotefancy.com/quote/1740418/Michelle-Akers-I-think-the-challenge-is-to-take-difficult-and-painful-times-and-turn-them.

"Alex Morgan." Encyclopedia Britannica, www.britannica.com/biography/Alex-Morgan.

"Alex Morgan." San Diego Wave FC, sandiegowavefc.com/player/alex-morgan/.

"Alex Morgan Quotes." QuoteFancy, quotefancy.com/alex-morgan-quotes.

Biography of Christine Sinclair." Christine Sinclair, christinesinclair.weebly.com/biography.html.

Biography.com Editors. "Hope Solo Biography." Biography.com, Biography.com, www.biography.com/athlete/hope-solo.

BrainyQuote. "Gianluigi Buffon Quotes." BrainyQuote, www.brainyquote.com/quotes/gianluigi_buffon_809461.

"Brazil women's star Marta to retire from international soccer." USA Today, 26 Apr. 2024, www.usatoday.com/story/sports/soccer/2024/04/26/brazil-womens-star-marta-to-retire-from-international-soccer/73468039007/.

BrainyQuote. "Alphonso Davies Quotes." BrainyQuote, www.brainyquote.com/authors/alphonso-davies-quotes.

BrainyQuote. "Frenkie de Jong Quotes." BrainyQuote, www.brainyquote.com/quotes/frenkie_de_jong_976808.

BrainyQuote. "Roberto Carlos Quotes." BrainyQuote, www.brainyquote.com/authors/roberto-carlos-quotes.

"Christine Sinclair." Canada Soccer, www.canadasoccer.com/profile/?id=2971&teamId=2089.

"Christine Sinclair Biography." TV Guide, www.tvguide.com/celebrities/christine-sinclair/bio/3030458236/.

"Christine Sinclair hopes custom Barbie will inspire next generation of athletes." Sportsnet, www.sportsnet.ca/soccer/article/christine-sinclair-hopes-custom-barbie-will-inspire-next-generation-of-athletes/.

"Christine Sinclair." Kiddle, kids.kiddle.co/Christine_Sinclair.

Davis, Gary. "What to Know About Mohamed Salah." OkayAfrica, OkayAfrica, 13 June 2018, https://www.okayafrica.com/what-to-know-about-mohamed-salah/.

Dewhurst, Sam. "What Does Mo Salah's Celebration Mean?" The Sun, 27 Dec. 2021, https://www.thesun.co.uk/sport/24894489/mo-salah-celebration-meaning/#:~:text=Mohamed%20Salah%20celebrates%20scoring%20some,and%20Asana%2C%20which%20means%20posture.

Donnellan, Katie. "Master of Strategy: Kevin De Bruyne's Tactical Influence on Manchester City's Game." A Football Report, 23 May 2021, https://afootballreport.com/blog/master-of-strategy-kevin-de-bruyne-s-tactical-influence-on-manchester-city-s-game#google_vignette.

Doyle, Tom. "13 Fun Facts About Kevin De Bruyne." Goal, Goal.com, 17 May 2021, https://www.goal.com/en-us/lists/13-fun-facts-about-kevin-de-bruyne/blt02c4e080a8fed912.

Doyle, Tom. "13 Fun Facts About Mohamed Salah." Goal, Goal.com, 17 May 2021, https://www.goal.com/en-us/lists/13-fun-facts-about-mohamed-salah/bltf99672bb845080a0.

ESPN. "Frenkie de Jong Player Profile." ESPN, www.espn.com/soccer/player/_/id/219022/frenkie-de-jong.

ExtraTime. "Gianluigi Buffon Player Profile." ExtraTime, www.extratime.com/player/11114294/gianluigi_buffon/#google_vig nette.

FBref. "Abby Wambach Player Profile." FBref, fbref.com/en/players/2d298b13/Abby-Wambach.

Fox Sports. "Weston McKennie Player Profile." Fox Sports, www.foxsports.com/soccer/weston-mckennie-player.

Frenkie de Jong Official Website. "Biography." Frenkie de Jong, www.frenkiedejong.com/en/biography/.

Girls Soccer Network. "Hope Solo: Best Keeper the USWNT Has Ever Seen?" Girls Soccer Network, girlssoccernetwork.com/hope-solo-best-keeper-the-uswnt-has-ever-seen/#:~=Years%20with%20the%20USWNT&text=In%20her%20c areer%20as%20a,the%20backbone%20of%20the%20USWNT.&text =Solo%20seemingly%20set%20the%20standard%20for%20American %20goalkeepers.

IMDb. "Gianluigi Buffon: Biography." IMDb, www.imdb.com/name/nm2308807/bio/.

IMDb. "Roberto Carlos: Biography." IMDb, www.imdb.com/name/nm0137784/bio/.

"Incredible Marta honoured with FIFA Special Award." FIFA, www.fifa.com/fifaplus/en/the-best-fifa-football-awards/articles/incredible-marta-honoured-with-special-award.

Jackson, Jamie. "Mohamed Salah Song: What Are the Lyrics to Liverpool Chant?" talkSPORT, talkSPORT, 20 Oct. 2021, https://talksport.com/football/660139/mohamed-salah-song-what-are-the-lyrics-to-liverpool-chant/.

Jobs in Football. "The Roberto Carlos Free Kick." Jobs in Football, jobsinfootball.com/blog/roberto-carlos-free-kick/.

"Kevin De Bruyne - Titles ; Achievements." Transfermarkt, https://www.transfermarkt.us/kevin-de-bruyne/erfolge/spieler/88755.

"Kevin De Bruyne." FBref.com, https://fbref.com/en/players/e46012d4/Kevin-De-Bruyne.

Kiddle. "Alphonso Davies." Kiddle, kids.kiddle.co/Alphonso_Davies.

Kiddle. "Gianluigi Buffon." Kiddle, kids.kiddle.co/Gianluigi_Buffon.

"Kylian Mbappé." Britannica Kids, kids.britannica.com/students/article/Kylian-Mbapp%C3%A9/636145#:~:text=Mbapp%C3%A9%20grew%20up%20in%20the,he%20was%20six%20years%20old.

"Kylian Mbappé." Encyclopædia Britannica, Encyclopædia Britannica, Inc., www.britannica.com/biography/Kylian-Mbappe.

"Kylian Mbappe Misses Playing Alongside Lionel Messi at PSG." ESPN, ESPN Internet Ventures, 15 Sept. 2022, www.espn.com/soccer/story/_/id/39246393/kylian-mbappe-misses-playing-alongside-lionel-messi-psg.

"Kylian Mbappé." Paris Saint-Germain Football Club, en.psg.fr/teams/first-team/squad/kylian-mbappe.

"Kylian Mbappé." Wikipedia, Wikimedia Foundation, en.wikipedia.org/wiki/Kylian_Mbapp%C3%A9.

"Kylian Mbappé Quotes." BrainyQuote, Xplore, www.brainyquote.com/quotes/kylian_mbappe_1056144.

"Lionel Messi." Olympics.com, olympics.com/en/athletes/lionel-messi.

"Lionel Messi Quotes." Encyclopedia Britannica, www.britannica.com/biography/Lionel-Messi.

Leo Messi Captains Fight Against Climate Change With 'Join The Planet'." Forbes, www.forbes.com/sites/vitascarosella/2024/03/06/leo-messi-captains-fight-against-climate-change-with-join-the-planet/?sh=48b289d460b8.

"Life's Work: An Interview with Megan Rapinoe." Harvard Business Review, hbr.org/2020/07/lifes-work-an-interview-with-megan-rapinoe.

Marta. Encyclopædia Britannica, Encyclopædia Britannica, Inc., www.britannica.com/biography/Marta.

Marta Quotes. BrainyQuote. Xplore, www.brainyquote.com/quotes/marta_653891.

"Megan Rapinoe." Team USA, www.teamusa.com/profiles/megan-rapinoe-876533.

"Megan Rapinoe Coming Under Fire." Newsweek, www.newsweek.com/megan-rapinoe-coming-under-fire-1843137.

"Megan Rapinoe's Farewell Game a Testament to Her Impact on LGBTQ Rights." Outsports, www.outsports.com/2023/9/25/23888869/megan-rapinoe-usa-uswnt-farewell-game-gay-lgbtq-rights/

"Megan Rapinoe Quotes." BrainyQuote, www.brainyquote.com/authors/megan-rapinoe-quotes.

"Michelle Akers." Encyclopaedia Britannica, www.britannica.com/biography/Michelle-Akers.

"Mia Hamm." Encyclopaedia Britannica, Encyclopaedia Britannica, Inc., https://www.britannica.com/biography/Mia-Hamm.

"Mia Hamm." My Hero, The MY HERO Project, https://myhero.com/m_hamm.

"Mia Hamm Quotes." BrainyQuote, https://www.brainyquote.com/authors/mia-hamm-quotes.

"Mohamed Salah." Encyclopaedia Britannica, Encyclopaedia Britannica, Inc., https://www.britannica.com/biography/Mohamed-Salah.

"Mohamed Salah." Encyclopaedia Britannica for Kids, Encyclopaedia Britannica, Inc., https://kids.britannica.com/students/article/Mohamed-Salah/631518.

"Mohamed Salah Quotes." BrainyQuote, https://www.brainyquote.com/quotes/mohamed_salah_917854.

Morgan, Alex. "Alex Morgan." Simon & Schuster, www.simonandschuster.com/authors/Alex-Morgan/409142853.

"Neymar Biography." Biography.com, A&E Television Networks, www.biography.com/athletes/neymar.

"Neymar." Encyclopædia Britannica, Encyclopædia Britannica, Inc., www.britannica.com/biography/Neymar.

"Neymar Jr." Neymar Jr Official Website, www.neymarjr.com/en/football.

"Neymar Jr. to Miss 2024 Copa America in United States Due to Injury, Brazil National Team Doctor Reveals." CBS Sports, CBS Interactive Inc., www.cbssports.com/soccer/news/neymar-jr-to-miss-2024-copa-america-in-united-states-due-to-injury-brazil-national-team-doctor-reveals/#:~:text=The%20Al%2DHilal%20forward%20has,nine%20months%20to%20recover%20fr

"Neymar Quotes." BrainyQuote, Xplore, www.brainyquote.com/quotes/neymar_845921.

OneFootball. "Top 5 Facts About Roberto Carlos That You Probably Didn't Know." OneFootball, onefootball.com/en/news/top-5-facts-about-roberto-carlos-that-you-probably-didnt-know-39122482.

Olympics.com. "Hope Solo Athlete Profile." Olympics.com, olympics.com/en/athletes/hope-solo.

"Pelé | Biography & Facts." Encyclopædia Britannica, Encyclopædia Britannica, Inc., 2024, www.britannica.com/biography/Pele-Brazilian-athlete.

"Pelé's Career, Stats and Records." South China Morning Post, 22 Mar. 2022, multimedia.scmp.com/infographics/sport/article/3208740/pele/index.html.

"Pelé Quotes." BrainyQuote, Xplore, www.brainyquote.com/authors/pele-quotes.

"Pelé Was the Epitome of Black Grace in Soccer." Andscape, andscape.com/features/pele-was-the-epitome-of-black-grace-in-soccer/.

"Pelé." Wikipedia, Wikimedia Foundation, 11 May 2024, en.wikipedia.org/wiki/Pel%C3%A9.

"Queen of Football: Marta." Goal, www.goal.com/story/queen-of-football-marta/index.html.

QuoteFancy. "Hope Solo Quotes." QuoteFancy, quotefancy.com/hope-solo-quotes

Real Madrid CF. "Roberto Carlos da Silva." Real Madrid CF, www.realmadrid.com/en-US/the-club/history/football-legends/roberto-carlos-da-silva.

Reddit. "LaLiga TV: Frenkie de Jong: 'I Think That with the Barcelona's Playing Style, I Can Fit In Very Well.'" Reddit, www.reddit.com/r/soccer/comments/1azp9fq/laliga_tv_frenkie_de_jong_i_think_that_with_the/.

Sinclair, Christine. "Christine Sinclair Quotes." BrainyQuote, www.brainyquote.com/quotes/christine_sinclair_545825.

Stenberg College. "Breaking Boundaries: Alphonso Davies' Journey from Buduburam Camp to Global Soccer Superstar." Stenberg College Blog, stenbergcollege.com/blog/breaking-boundaries-alphonso-davies-journey-from-buduburam-camp-to-global-soccer-superstar/.

"Sterett, Bill. 'High-Level ACL Repair.' Dr. Sterett, www.drsterett.com/sports-medicine-blog/high-level-acl-repair."

Stokstad, Eliza. "How Did Mia Hamm Inspire Women to Play Sports?" Smithsonian American Women's History Museum, 17 Aug. 2021, https://womenshistory.si.edu/blog/how-did-mia-hamm-inspire-women-play-sports#:~:text=At%2015%20years%20old%2C%20she,the%20University%20of%20North%20Carolina.

Taylor, Daniel. "Kevin De Bruyne: 'Every Time I Lose I Feel I Could Have Done Something Better'." The Guardian, Guardian News and Media, 26 Nov. 2022, https://www.theguardian.com/football/2022/nov/26/kevin-de-bruyne-manchester-city-belgium-world-cup-home-life

TV Guide. "Abby Wambach: Bio." TV Guide, www.tvguide.com/celebrities/abby-wambach/bio/3000396831/.

TV Guide. "Gianluigi Buffon: Bio." TV Guide, www.tvguide.com/celebrities/gianluigi-buffon/bio/3030290551/.

The18. "The Weston McKennie Story." The18, the18.com/en/soccer-news/national-peanut-board/weston-mckennie-story..

The Football HQ. "Frenkie de Jong: One of the World's Best, 4 Years in the Making." Medium, The Football HQ, 8 Dec. 2023, thefootballhq.medium.com/frenkie-de-jong-one-of-the-worlds-best-4-years-in-the-making-b6b070831870.

The New York Times. "Frenkie de Jong Analysed: Barcelona's Rising Star, in His Own Words." The New York Times, www.nytimes.com/athletic/3401831/2022/09/12/frenkie-de-jong-analysed-barcelona/.

"Top 10 Kevin De Bruyne Quotes." BrainyQuote, https://www.brainyquote.com/lists/authors/top-10-kevin-de-bruyne-quotes.

"Top Facts About Lionel Messi." PureVPN, www.purevpn.com/blog/top-facts-about-lionel-messi/.

UCF Knights. "Michelle Akers." UCF Knights Women's Soccer, ucfknights.com/sports/womens-soccer/roster/season/2009-10/staff/michelle-akers.

U.S. Soccer. "Weston McKennie Player Profile." U.S. Soccer, www.ussoccer.com/players/m/weston-mckennie.

Us Weekly. "Hope Solo's Ups and Downs Through the Years: DUI, More." Us Weekly, www.usmagazine.com/celebrity-news/pictures/hope-solos-ups-and-downs-through-the-years-dui-more/.

Vancouver Whitecaps FC. "Alphonso Davies Player Profile." Vancouver Whitecaps FC, www.whitecapsfc.com/players/alphonso-davies/.

Vulpuk. "Weston McKennie Update." Vulpuk, vulpuk.blob.core.windows.net/updatein/weston-mckennie.html

Wambach, Abby. "About Abby Wambach." Abby Wambach Official Website, abbywambach.com/about/.

Wikipedia. "Alphonso Davies." Wikipedia, en.wikipedia.org/wiki/Alphonso_Davies.

Wikipedia. "Roberto Carlos." Wikipedia, en.wikipedia.org/wiki/Roberto_Carlos.

Wise, Mike. "Ham, Foudy, Lilly, Fawcett - They Have Starred for More than a Decade." The Washington Post, 8 June 1999, https://www.washingtonpost.com/wp-srv/sports/soccer/longterm/worldcup99/articles/cupus4.htm#:~:text=Hamm%2C%20Foudy%2C%20Lilly%2C%20Fawcett,for%20more%20than%20a%20decade."

"Zinedine Zidane." Daily Mail, www.dailymail.co.uk/sport/zinedine-zidane/index.html.

"Zinedine Zidane." Encyclopædia Britannica, Encyclopædia Britannica, Inc., www.britannica.com/biography/Zinedine-Zidane.

"Zinedine Zidane." FBref.com, FBref.com, fbref.com/en/players/654f4e63/Zinedine-Zidane.

"Zinedine Zidane." Real Madrid Official Website, www.realmadrid.com/en-US/the-club/history/football-legends/zinedine-zidane.

"Zinedine Zidane Quotes." BrainyQuote, Xplore, www.brainyquote.com/quotes/zinedine_zidane_479437.

Made in the USA
Columbia, SC
01 July 2025

60196767R00107